Polish Tracks & W

Adam Jońca

Renault FT-17/NC1/NC2/TSF
Renault R35/40
Hotchkiss H35/39

French tanks in the Polish Army

STRATUS

Published in Poland in 2009
by STRATUS s.c.
Po. Box 123,
27-600 Sandomierz 1, Poland
e-mail: office@mmpbooks.biz
for
Mushroom Model Publications,
36 Ver Road, Redbourn,
AL3 7PE, UK.
e-mail: rogerw@mmpbooks.biz
© 2009 Mushroom Model
Publications.
http://www.mmpbooks.biz

All rights reserved. Apart from any fair dealing for the purpose of private study, research, criticism or review, as permitted under the Copyright, Design and Patents Act, 1988, no part of this publication may be reproduced, stored in a retrieval system, or transmitted in any form or by any means, electronic, electrical, chemical, mechanical, optical, photocopying, recording or otherwise, without prior written permission. All enquiries should be addressed to the publisher.

**ISBN
978-83-61421-01-6**

Editor in chief
Roger Wallsgrove

Editorial Team
Bartłomiej Belcarz
Robert Pęczkowski
Artur Juszczak

Colour Drawings
Adam Jońca

Concept of layout
Bartłomiej Belcarz
Artur Bukowski

Layout
Artur Bukowski

Cocver
Artur Juszczak

Cover design
Maciej Kowalski

Translation
Artur Przęczek

Proof reading
Roger Wallsgrove
Dick Taylor

DTP
Artur Bukowski

Printed by
Drukarnia Diecezjalna,
ul. Żeromskiego 4,
27-600 Sandomierz
tel. +48 (15) 832 31 92
fax +48 (15) 832 77 87
www.wds.pl
marketing@wds.pl

PRINTED IN POLAND

Table of contents

From France to Poland 3
    Martigny les Bains 3
Between the wars 16
    Reorganizations 16
    French episode 22
    FT-17 tanks in Polish Army 1920-1939 Gallery 23
    CWS tanks 34
    TSF tanks 41
    Smoke screen tank 42
    Armoured rail vehicles 43
    Attempts to modernise FT-17 tanks 47
    M 26/27 tanks 49
    NC1 tank 51
September of 1939 53
    Renault FT-17 in September campaign of 1939 53
    12th Armoured Battalion 65
    21 Light Tank Battalion 66
    Half company of Lieutenant Jakubowicz 70
Soldiers and tanks of General Maczek 73
    Coëtquidan 73
    In the Rodan valley 74
    Near Paris 85
    10 Brygada Kawalerii 86
Badges 96

Photographs from author's collection and collections of Bogusław Bobel, Zbigniew Cheda, Pascal Danjou, Zofia Górska, Jacek Haber, Tomasz Kopański, Krzysztof Kuryłowicz, Zbyszek Lalak, Janusz Magnuski, Wawrzyniec Markowski, Witold Rawski, Thierre Vallet; and archives from Instytut Gen. Sikorskiego (The Polish Institute and Sikorski Museum) – special thanks to Krzysztof Barbarski and Krzysztof Gebhard, Archiwum Dokumentacji Mechanicznej, Dom Spotkań z Historią, Muzeum Wojska Polskiego, Ośrodek Karta.

Get in picture!
Do you have photographs of historical aircraft, airfields in action, or original and unusual stories to tell? MMP would like to hear from you! We welcome previously unpublished material that will help to make MMP books the best of their kind. We will return original photos to you and provide full credit for your images. Contact us before sending us any valuable material: rogerw@mmpbooks.biz

Media partner in Poland
Historical magazin "Do Broni"
ZP-Group sp. z o.o.
Smolikowskiego 6/8, 00-389 Warszawa
www.dobroni.pl

From France to Poland

Martigny les Bains

On 22 March 1919 the French 505 Tank Regiment *(505 Régiment des Chars Blindés)* stationed at Martigny les Bains in the Vosges Department, began its transformation into the Polish 1st Tank Regiment *(1 Pułk Czołgów / 1-er Régiment des Chars Blindés Polonais)*. The newly formed Polish unit obtained all the equipment and armament, but large part of the personnel remained French. The regiment retained its commander, most of the French officers and non-commissioned officers, as well as many tank drivers and gunners. The auxiliary sections consisting of the repair workshop and transportation units also kept most of their original staff.

1st Tank Regiment was created by the order of Polish Army Command in France *(Dowództwo Armii Polskiej we Francji)*. Polish Army in France was established by President Raymond Poincare as means of extending the coalition of nations fighting the Central Powers. The decree regulating this matter was signed on 4 June 1917.

By 1 May 1919, 1 *Pułk Czołgów* was fully organized. It consisted of five tank companies numbered 1, 2, 3, 6 and 7. This numerical sequence corresponded with numbers of Polish infantry divisions stationed in France, infantry divisions 4 and 5 were in Russia at the time. Tank companies, just like their French counterparts, had 24 Renault FT-17 tanks. Each company consisted of three platoons equipped with five tanks. Three of the tanks had 37 mm cannon *(char canon)*, the remaining two tanks had a Hotchkiss machine gun *(char mitrailleuse)*. The company also had 9 tanks in the echelon platoon, one company commander tank, and possibly some additional, non regulation, spare tanks. The auxiliary support of the regiment consisted of transport and repair sections. Transport section was equipped with a passenger car, trucks and tractors. Repair section had mobile workshops on truck chassis, as well as parts supply storage. All together the regiment had 120 tanks, 41 vehicles, 7 tractors, 10 motorcycles.

First Polish volunteers begun to arrive in the regiment as early as March 1919. Some were Polish nationality prisoners of war from the German and Austro – Hungarian armies. Others were volunteers from Polish emigrant families residing in France and USA. The 1st Company was formed almost exclusively form the latter.

[1]: The Renault factory emblem. This cast iron plaque was riveted to the suspension beam of the Renault FT-17 tank.

[2]: Renault FT-17 on a flat rail wagon - arrival of the 1st Tank Regiment from France to Poland, June 1919.

ŁÓDŹ

On the 1 June 1919 the first railway transports carrying the Tank Regiment arrived into Łódź. This day was later celebrated as a regimental anniversary. At the time of transfer to Poland, the 1st Regiment consisted of 388 Frenchmen, including 34 officers, and 453 Poles, including 11 officers.

Seventeen more Polish officers were added to the regimental personnel during June. The regiment's commander was Lieutenant Colonel (*podpułkownik*) Jules Maré. He previously commanded the 505 Tank Regiment, his French Army rank was Major (*commandante*). The liaison officer (*L'adjutant des Regiments*) was Major E. d'Armancourt, his French rank was captain (*capitaine*).

At first, the regiment was organized into two battalions numbered I and III. The III Battalion was soon renumbered II. The I Battalion, originally French 15th Battalion of the 505 Regiment, consisted of the 1st Company (originally French 343), and the 2nd Company (French 344). The III Battalion (French 14th Battalion) included 5th Company (French 340), 6th Company (French 341)

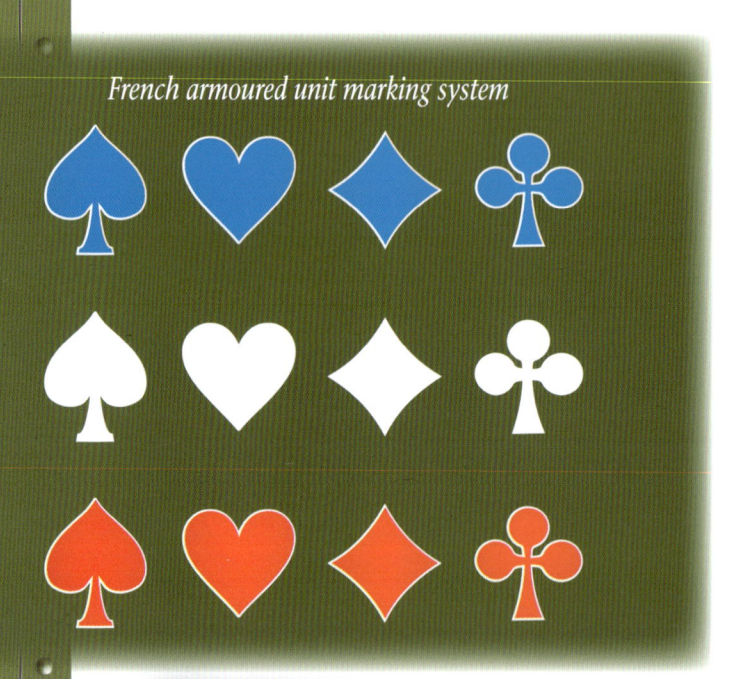

French armoured unit marking system

[3]: Colour and insignia:
1st Company – blue
2nd Company – white
3rd Company – red
1st Platoon (section) – spades
2nd Platoon (section) – hearts
3rd Platoon (section) – diamonds
4th Platoon (section) – clubs
In battle conditions the markings were sometimes obscured. In order to improve visibility a white outline was later used for blue and red. At a later time, some units had their emblems painted inside a white geometrical shape. Circle, square, and a triangle were used for the 1st, 2nd and 3rd companies respectively. For obvious reason, the 2nd company emblems had to be painted against a darker background.

[4]: FT-17 tanks in Rembertów photograph taken in Rembertów on 2 November 1919.

[5]: *French tanker's badge emblem worn on a regulation beret. In the 1st Tank Regiment this practice was most likely limited to French personnel. The badges are not vident in photographs taken after 1920.*

[6]: *The 1st Regiment tank bearing "Passe par tout" on the turret. Towards the rear of the hull, an emblem of the 2nd Platoon of the I Company, on the sides number 470. It is uncertain if this number had any relevance, or was it just an old French numerical. The playing card symbols, used as an insignia of companies and their respective platoons, were inherited with the tanks and often disregarded, some tanks had them, and some did not. The tank has a tri - colour camouflage scheme, without contour lines.*

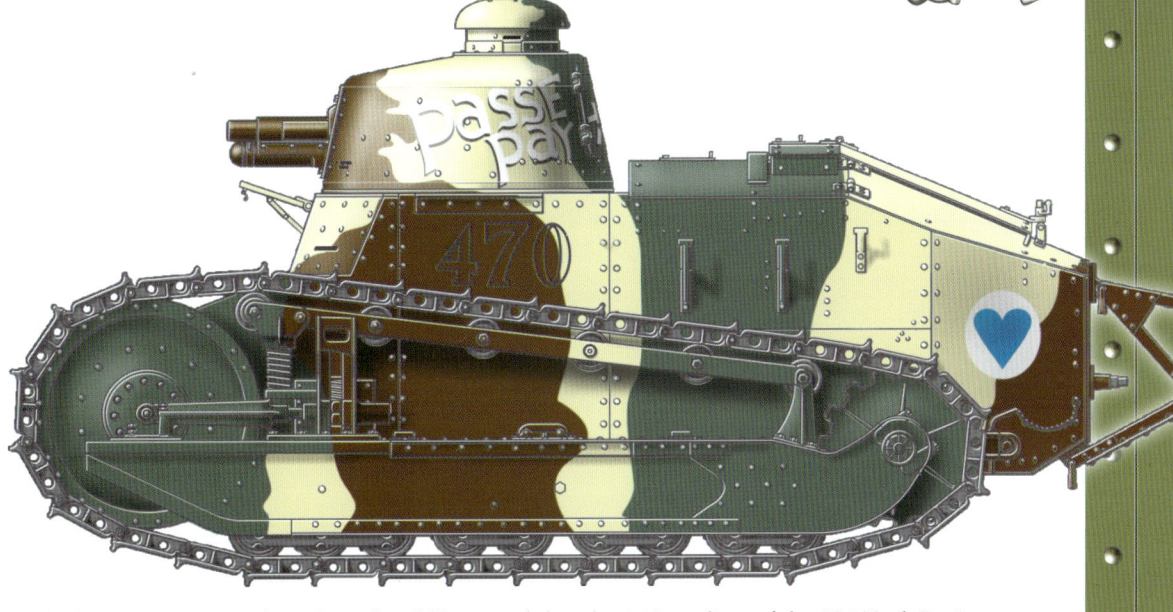

and 7th Company (French 342). It should be noted that the 16 Battalion of the 505 Tank Regiment never underwent a transformation. It remained intact in the French Army and was used to recreate the entire Tank Regiment, after the Polish unit had departed. Shortly the III battalion was renamed the II and its Companies became 3 and 4 respectively.

The 1st Tank Regiment was commanded by French officers until October 1919, while Polish officers were acting as doubles throughout the chain of command. After that time the unit become almost exclusively Polish with the exception of French officers and non-commissioned officers acting as advisors and trainers. Lieutenant Colonel Maré, formally an attaché of the French Military Mission (*Mission Militaire Francaise*), took part in all the military actions until the defence of Warsaw in the later phase of the war. Majors Vigneron and Peeré acted as advisors for the duration of the Polish-Soviet war. Captain Brun stayed with the 1st Regiment until 1926.

[7]: *Renault FT-17s of the 1st Tank Regiment – photograph most likely taken during the presentation of tanks at Rembertów near Warsaw, summer 1919.*

[8]: Presentation of FT-17 tank in Rembertów, summer 1919.

[9]: Renault FT-17 of the 1st Tank Regiment – photograph most likely taken during the presentation of equipment at Rembertów near Warsaw, summer 1919.

[10]: Renault FT-17 tanks near the front, probably 6 August 1920 near Warsaw. The first tank is named "Adela".

[11]: The tank named "Anicia" – Haller Army officer standing by the tank.

[12]: The tank named "Junona".

[13]: Crew and their tank with red heart symbol, emblem of the 2nd Platoon of the III Company.

[14]: Front lines year 1920. The tank "Lis" (Fox) with number 1639.

[15]: The 1st Regiment tanks after unloading from the train in the vicinity of the front lines in 1920.

1st Tank Regiment in action

The Polish – Soviet war became imminent from 18 November 1918. Leo Trockij, a member of the Bolshevik Council of the People's Commissars, had announced that the Bolshevik revolution must be spread West. It presented a grave threat to the newly re-emerged Polish Republic as this drive was declared a necessity, and to be done over the corpse of bourgeois Poland. As the war escalated, in March 1919 the front extended from the Belarusian town of Kobryń to the Niemen River. In July, after a Polish victory over the Ukrainians in East Galicia, the extents of the front included the province of Wołyń and Zbrucz River.

The I Battalion was placed at the disposal of General Szeptycki, the commander of the North – West Front also known as Lithuanian – Belarus Front *(Front Litewsko – Białoruski)*. The tanks had

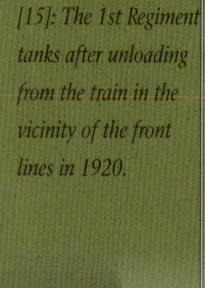

[16]: The 1st Regiment tanks unloaded from the rail transport near the front lines in 1920.

[17]: "Lis" (Fox). Tri colour, also referred to as three tone camouflage, some of the patches have black outlines. Nunber 1639.

[18]: Year 1920. The 1st Regiment tanks in the vicinity of the front, unloaded from the railroad wagons.

[19]: Year 1920. The 1st Regiment tanks in the vicinity of the front, unloaded from the railroad wagons.

their first engagement on 19 August 1919. The 2nd Company of the I Battalion, together with the repair and transportation platoon, supported the advancement of the 14 Wielkopolska Infantry Division on Bobrujsk. At the end of September, the same company had lost two of its tanks in heavy fighting near Dynenburg (Daugavpils). During that time the 2nd Company fought under the command of French Captain Durfur, the platoon commanders were also French and the crews mixed. The I Battalion was kept in reserve of the North-West Front and its 1st Company was stationed at Wilno (Vilnius). Towards the end of October of 1919, the 2nd Company was also moved

[20]: Tanks at the South-Eastern front around 1920. The tank on the left has a painting on its turret, a white skull and bones emblem accompanied by the name "Trup" (The Corps). The tank next to it, has the name "Maryśa" painted on a spare track link.

[21]: FT-17 and its French commander at Dynenburg.

to Wilno after being recalled from the front. By the first half of 1920 the personnel of the 1st Tank Regiment was strictly Polish.

At the beginning of July 1920 the 1st Company took part in the defence of Wilno. After its collapse, the tanks were evacuated via rail to Lida. On the 17 July 1920 the 1st Company was fighting in defence of the town. The tanks remained on the railway flatcars, and were utilized as an improvised armoured train. The objective was to hold the station until the arrival of two Polish armoured trains, "Boruta" and "Lis-Kula".

Later, all three trains, the tanks of the 1st Company still as an improvised armoured train, cooperated in actions against the Soviets. After the retreat from Lida, the 1st Company was directed to

[22]: Turret of a machine gun tank, referred to as the char mitrailleuse. The skull and bones emblem painted in white was unique to this tank, named "The Corpse" (Trup).

Grodno, there it met with the II Battalion Headquarters and the 2nd Company of the I Battalion. At Grodno both companies participated in heavy fighting. During the evacuation, three tanks were lost as a result of an otherwise successful attempt to break out of Bolshevik sack. After the fall of Grodno, the 2nd Company took part in a counterattack. As a result, one of the forts and the south bank of the Niemen River were recaptured from the enemy. From 20 to 26 July, the tanks of the 2nd Company on its own tracks, and the 1st Company on the railcars, participated in covering the retreat of the Polish forces. After reaching the town of Sokółka, the tanks of the 2nd Company had to be transferred by train to Łódź in order to conduct the necessary inspections, maintenance and repairs.

The 1st Company participated in the Polish defence, delaying the pursuit of Soviet forces near Białystok, defending the Narwa River bridge at Łapy on 29 through 30 July. From 3 August the company was used as a rear guard at Łomża, and later at Długosiodło, Wyszków and Tłuszcz.

[23]: Improvised armoured train – a regulation flat railcar of former Prussian Railways, still with German markings. The tank on the left in typical tri – colour camouflage with contour outlines and the clubs insignia of the 1st Platoon of the 3 Company, number unknown. The tank on the right in the similar camouflage scheme, but without contour lines, has French registration number 66658.

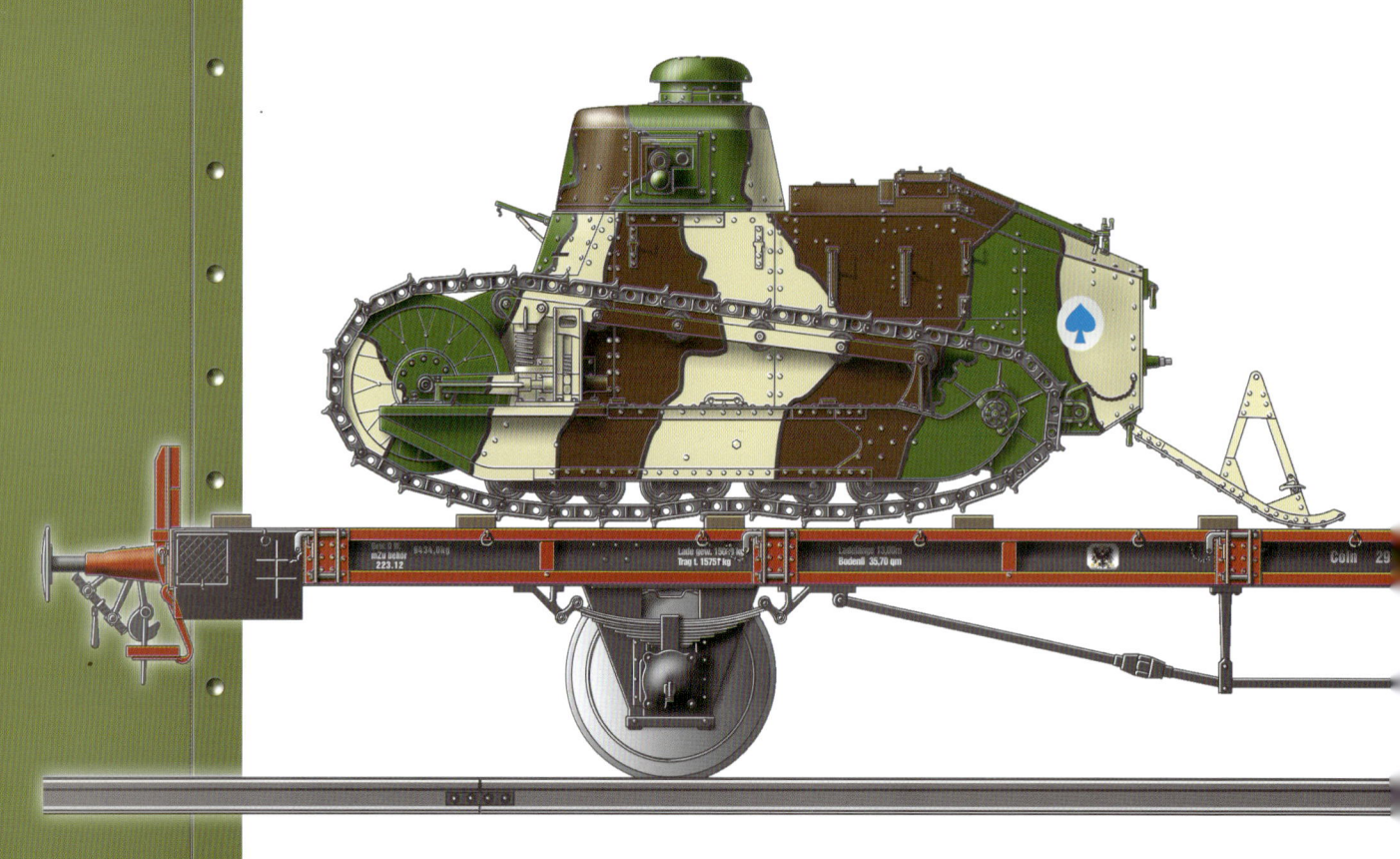

The II Tank Battalion was a reserve formation at the Ukrainian Front from the beginning of 1920. In the second half of May 1920 the 3rd Company was stationed in Kijów *(Київ)*. The company was mostly active in the skirmishes and reconnaissance on the approaches leading to Kijów. The company was moved to Koziatyn *(Козятин)* after Soviet cavalry broke through Polish defences on 31 May. Meanwhile II Battalion Headquarters and the 4th Company were relocated to Koziatyn from Łódź. Both companies took part in the defence of the Koziatyn railway centre on 5 and 6 June. Nine disabled tanks were loaded on flat railcars and formed yet another improvised armoured train. The 3rd Company cooperated with infantry from 6 to 10 June, and later covered the retreat. On July 22, both companies were concentrated near Płoskirów. The dire situation at the front prevented the scheduled transfer of the 3rd Company to Łódź for maintenance and repairs. Instead, on 3 and 4 of July the company fought advancing soviet cavalry near Zdołbunowo. On 4 July, the 1st, 2nd and 3rd Platoons of the 4th Company, in constant contact with the advancing enemy, reached Równe. Here again, a provisional armoured train on railway flatcars was formed. The platoons were involved in covering the retreat and evacuation of Równe. Facing shortages of fuel and ammunitions the tanks were nonetheless able to regroup at the railway station. The enemy forces, preoccupied with plunder and ransack of the city, did not pursue. This allowed loading the tanks onto an abandoned train and withdrawal towards Kostopol. After the Równe encounter 12 tanks of the 4th Company were in need of repair, so they were accordingly relocated to allow for this. The remainder of the 4th Company did not participate in further fighting, and in mid August it was located near Warsaw.

In August 1920 only 33 Renault FT-17 tanks participated in bringing the Soviet offensive towards Warsaw to a standstill. The 3rd Company was engaged at Lwów, while the 1st Company repaired their tanks in Łódź.

On 15 August, the day of so-called Miracle at the Vistula (*Cud nad Wisłą*), two platoons of the newly-formed 5th Company of the III Battalion fought at Radzymin. In the afternoon of the same day, 1st Platoon of the 4th Company participated in the counterattack towards Okuniew.

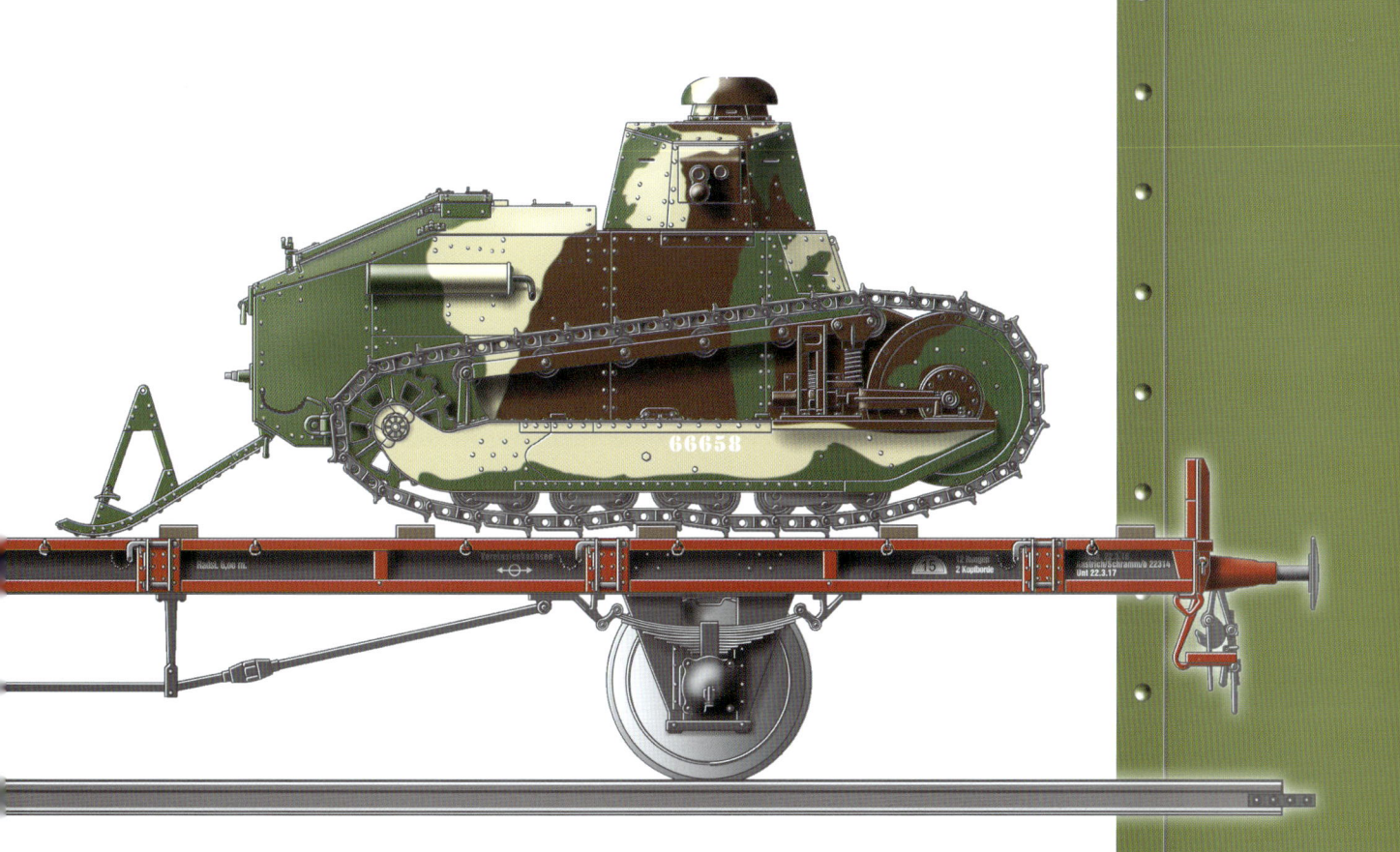

[24]: Year 1920, Renault tank crossing a water obstacle. The photograph was most likely taken during one of many propaganda exhibitions held at the time.

[25]: Polish tank on a platform at Równe railway station.

The fierce battle at Radzymin was a turning point which allowed for the massive Polish counteroffensive. As the critical situation was defused, an Armoured Group *(Grupa Pancerna)* was formed in order to lead a swift thrust of Polish forces towards Mińsk Mazowiecki. This temporary formation consisted of two platoons of the 2nd Tank Company, one platoon of the 4th Company and two platoons of the 5th Company, as well as three armoured trains "Danuta", "Mściciel" and "Paderewski". The second assignment of the Group was to take Przasnysz, and than reach Mława. The composition of the Armoured Group was altered, armoured train "Mściciel" was withdrawn, while "Hallerczyk", "Lis-Kula", and two improvised armoured trains were added. Each of the improvised trains consisted of five Renault FT-17 tanks on flat railcars. Armoured train "Danuta" with the support of improvised ones, captured Mława railway station on August 21. The tanks did not participate in further fighting, lack of fuel forced them to stay in Mława. On August 26 all the units of Armoured Group, with the exception of armoured train "Hallerczyk", returned to Warsaw. On the same day the 4th Company received an order of dispatch to Lublin. The tanks were positioned in platoon formations at the main approaches to the town.

The Renault tanks did not participate in any more actions, they remained as a reserve formation at the disposal of the Main Command *(Naczelne Dowództwo)* until armistice. The I Battalion was stationed in Lwów, II Battalion in Białystok, III

Battalion along with the 1st Regiment command, reserve company, and repair section returned to Łódź.

The bravery and devotion of the tank crews were reflected by the number of military decorations awarded. The highest Polish decoration, Virtuti Militari Cross *(Krzyż Virtuti Militari)* was awarded 34 times, the Cross of Valor *(Krzyż Walecznych)* 31 times. Jules Maré, promoted to the rank of colonel, received one Virtuti Militari Cross and one Cross of Valor. Major A. Marchand received a Cross of Valor.

[26]: *Tanks on the street at Mińsk Mazowiecki, 17 August 1920.*

[27]: *Year 1920, Renault tanks at Mokotowskie Field (Pole Mokotowskie) Warsaw.*

Between the wars

Reorganizations

In the winter of 1920, after several changes of location, all the battalions of the Tank Regiment were placed in permanent garrisons. The I Battalion, at the time of armistice stationed in Lwów, was moved to Warsaw. The II Battalion, moved from Bialystok, via Kraków, was finally stationed in Żurawica near Przemyśl. As of early January 1921 the III Battalion was in Biedrusk. In November it was transferred to Poznan, which became its permanent garrison town. The main headquarters, the reserve battalion, and the workshops remained in Łódz.

In August of 1921 the Tank Regiment was dissolved as a formation, while the battalions were granted a status of independent units. At the same time a Central Tank Academy (*Centralna Szkoła Czołgów*) was established in Warsaw. After the Silesian plebiscite an independent tank company was temporarily created. Two platoons devolved from the II and the III Battalions were stationed in Katowice at the end of 1921. After two months, the unit was disbanded and the tanks returned to their respective battalions.

The 1st Tank Regiment was reinstated in February of 1923. It was assigned to a garrison at Żurawica. The Central Tank Academy and the I Battalion were also transferred to this location. In January of the following year, the III Battalion was transferred to Żurawica as well. In 1925 the third company was added to each of the, so far two company, battalions.

In October of 1930, the regiment had moved to Poznan, while the II Battalion and the workshops remained in Żurawica. In July of 1931 the regiment was renamed 1st Armoured Regiment (*1 Pułk Pancerny*). The II Tank Battalion in conjunction with 2nd Armoured Car Regiment (*2 Dywizjon Samochodów Pancernych*) became the 2nd Armoured Regiment. Subsequent reorganization of armoured forces again transformed the regiments into independent battalions. Beginning in 1935, additional armoured battalions were created. By that time, the history of the Renault tank in Poland was almost solely associated with the II Battalion at Żurawica, now known as the 2nd Armoured Battalion (*2 Batalion Pancerny*). This unit was absorbing all the Renault tanks replaced with newer equipment in other battalions.

The number of Renault tanks, at one time nearing 200, was steadily diminishing due to mechanical wear. According to the report dated 11 July 1936, there were 174 tanks available. This number

[28]: Renault FT-17 tanks at the Biedrusk proving ground around 1930.

[29]: Military parade on Warszawska street in Katowice, 22 of June 1922. The parade was organized to commemorate the incorporation of Upper Silesia into Poland. The tank in the front bears a female name "Stacha".

[30]: Another snap shot of the parade. The tank behind "Stacha" is named "Salcia". The 23rd Field Artillery Regiment marches on, displaying the French 75 mm Schneider 1897 guns obtained two month prior to this military review.

[31]: 27 February 1921, tank show in Poznań.

[32]: Pontoon bridge at Biedrusk, 23 May 1931.

[33]: Tank Battalion from Żurawica on Mickiewicza Street in Przemyśl.

[34]: Tanks crossing the pontoon bridge. Biedrusk, 23 May 1931.

[35]: The 1st Regiment tanks in formation ready for a parade in Poznań, 11 March 1933. The armoured car in the front is probably an unarmed parade vehicle with loudspeakers. The chassis remains unknown. Contrary to some sources, it is not a Berliet vehicle.

[36]: 11 March 1933. Military review in front of the monument of Christ The King founded by the citizens of Poznań. The monument was erected one year earlier to commemorate independence.

[37]: Tanks at Biedrusk proving ground. On the left, a Renault CWS tank number 3002 manufactured at Central Vehicle Shops. In the distance, prototype "M" tank with narrow link track.

[38]: Military review at Biedrusk, 6 August 1934.

[39]: Renault tanks in motion; around 1930.

[40]: The 1st Regiment tanks during parade in Poznań, 1933.

[41]: Column of Polish CWS tanks, October 1927.

included 112 Renault FT-17 tanks, numbered 1001 – 1112; 6 TSF tanks, numbered 2001 – 2006; 29 other Renault tanks, numbered 1113 – 1142 (this group included the NC, as well as the FT-17 tanks); one NC1 tank, number 1153, and 27 CWS training tanks, numbered 3001 – 3027. A small number of FT-17 tanks was sold to Spain, but shortly before the outbreak of the Second World War no one else was interested in their purchase. As of 15 July 1939, the 2nd Armoured Battalion had 51 tanks as a mobilization reserve "a", 7 exercise tanks (*czołg ćwiczebny*) subjected to mobilization, and 12 training tanks (*czołg szkolny*). Apart from that, the 1st Armoured Trains Regiment (*1 Dywizjon Pociągów Pancernych*) had 10 mobilization reserve tanks, 4 exercise tanks, and 2 training tanks. The 2nd Armoured Train Regiment had 7 reserve, 7 exercise, and 2 training tanks.

[42]: Birds eye view of Żurawica.

French episode

The account of the Renault tank in Poland would be incomplete without a mention of one more event.

In 1921, after the violent dispute over Upper Silesia, the Inter-Allied Commission of Control (*La Commission Interalliée de Gouvernement et de Plébiscite de Haute-Silésie*) was forced to take over the government of the region and arrange for the plebiscite. In order to control unrest and maintain order, allied forces were dispatched to form an expedition corps.

Part of this military contingent was French 46 Alpine Troop Division, Italian 135 Alpine Troop Regiment, and four British reinforced infantry battalions.

General Jules Gratier, the commanding officer of this corps, also had an armoured company at his disposal. The company had 3 sections, stationed in Katowice, Bytom and Opole. The armament consisted of 18 armoured cars and 26 Renault FT-17 tanks. It was not always a peaceful mission. On few occasions, the unit stationed in Katowice was involved in the exchange of fire with German militia forces.

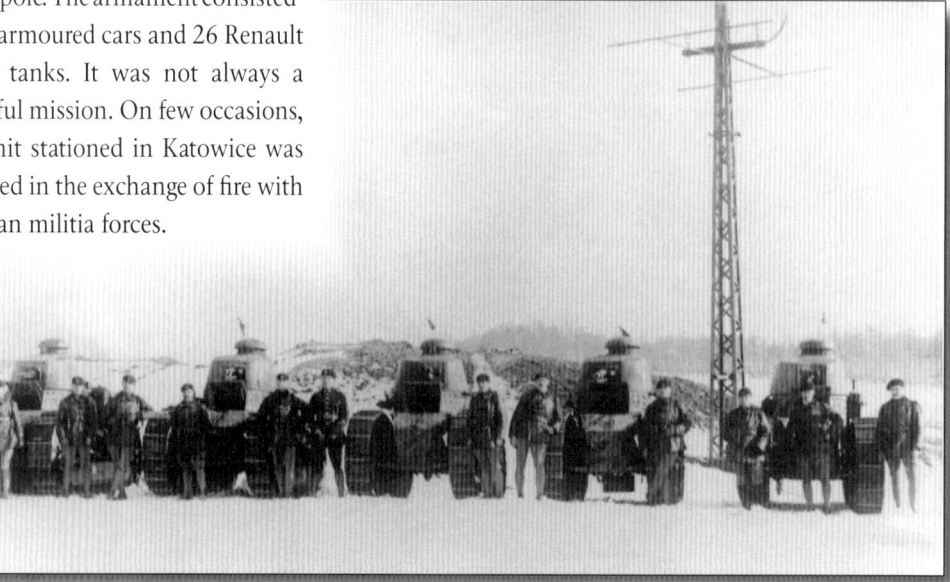

[43]: French tank on the streets of Katowice.

[44]: A platoon of French tanks in Opole.

[45]: French tanks in Bytom.

FT-17 tanks in Polish Army 1920-1939 Gallery

[46]: Renault tank with unidentified number. The photograph is from an earlier period, prior to introduction of Polish markings. Camouflage is most likely tri- colour, with black contour lines. Above the heart emblem, white number 4. The circle under the heart is outlined in a darker colour, it is uncertain if it had any meaning, or was it just done for esthetical purposes.

[47]: Renault FT-17 tank number 1005 on a proving grounds around 1930.

[48]: Another photograph of Renault FT-17 tank number 1005 on proving grounds around 1930.

[49]: Renault FT-17 number 1008 photographed at Żurawica. The tank has a riveted, octagonal turret composed of flat armour plates. Such turrets were less frequently encountered among Polish tanks; the cast turret was predominant. The vehicle marking is uncommon; the repetitive placement of the number on the turret is rarely seen on surviving photographs.

[50]: Tank number 1009, around 1930.

[51]: Tank number 1009 and tank 10143, Biedrusk around 1930.

[52]: Tank number 1013, around 1930.

[53]: Tank number 1028. The photograph was taken towards the end of the 1920s. French tri-colour camouflage without contour lines.

[54]: Tank number 1019, around 1930.

[55]: Tank number 1029, late '20s.

[56]: Polish armoured vehicle recognition signs introduced in the 1930s. The geometric figures were painted on metal panels. At the top, the company commander symbol. Below, the platoon symbols. Circle – 1st platoon, triangle – 2nd platoon, square – 3rd platoon. The vertical stripe, painted in red, specified the platoon commander. The red circle, according to some sources, indicated the reserve vehicle of a platoon. Other sources state that the markings were reserved for the second in command officer. All other tanks had white geometric figures painted against olive-green background.

[57]: Tank number 1033, early '30s.

[58]: Renault FT-17 number 1034, during infantry review in 1930.

[59]: Tank number 1047, during infantry review in 1930.

[60]: Tank number 1047.

[61]: Tank number 1047, during infantry review in 1930.

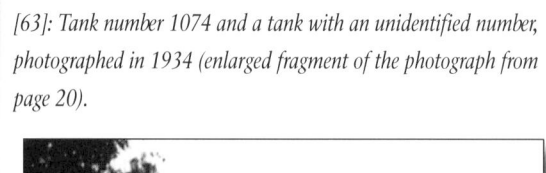

[62]: Tank number 1076, early '30s.

[63]: Tank number 1074 and a tank with an unidentified number, photographed in 1934 (enlarged fragment of the photograph from page 20).

[64]: Tank number 1078 during a military parade in Warsaw.

[65]: Tank number 1087 in Warsaw during the May coup d'état (Przewrót Majowy) in May 1926. Before driving out onto the streets of Warsaw, the tank was probably under maintenance or repair. Numbers are hand painted, or written with the use of chalk. French camouflage may be noted. The tank is missing the regulation tools and accessories.

[66]: Tank number 1097 performing an exercise with infantry, during Wołyń manoeuvres in August 1925.

[67]: Tank number 1099 at Biedrusk proving ground in 1929.

[68]: Renault FT-17 number 1102 during manoeuvres at Stanisławów in 1925.

[69]: Another photograph of Renault FT-17 number 1102 during manoeuvres at Stanisławów in 1925.

[70]: Renault FT-17 number 1102 during manoeuvres at Stanisławów in 1925.

[71]: At times, it is difficult to identify the tanks, as illustrated by these two photographs. On the left, a 1st Battalion tank photographed on 27 April 1927. On the second photograph, a tank without the identifying number usually painted on the suspension beam. The only information available about this photograph is that it was taken in March 1933 at Poznań.

33

CWS TANKS

Initially, there was a plan to produce Renault FT-17 tanks in Poland. As the retirement of the tanks from active roster become apparent, the production plans were abandoned. Nonetheless, the Central Vehicle Shops (*Centralne Warsztaty Samochodowe*) did construct a number of FT-17 tanks. The tanks were built to French specifications and technical documentation, with the use of original French spare parts. Due to production techniques, there were minor departures from the typical construction of FT-17. The main difference was that the CWS tanks were constructed using ordinary, non hardened, steel plates. The tanks were intended for training and exercise purposes, allowing the original FT-17 to remain combat ready. There were probably 27 CWS tanks, numbered 3001-3027, but this is not certain. Some CWS tanks could differ from the others, due to a series of experiments and modification attempts.

[72]: The CWS emblem. The metal emblem was affixed to the front plate of the Renault FT-17 tanks build at Polish Central Vehicle Shops (Centralne Warsztaty Samochodowe).

[73]: Tank number 3001 exercising at Modlin, around 1930.

[74]: Tank number 3001 transported on Renault FU truck number 6939, crossing the bridge.

[75]: Tank number 3002 (enlarged fragment of the photograph from page 19 and page 21).

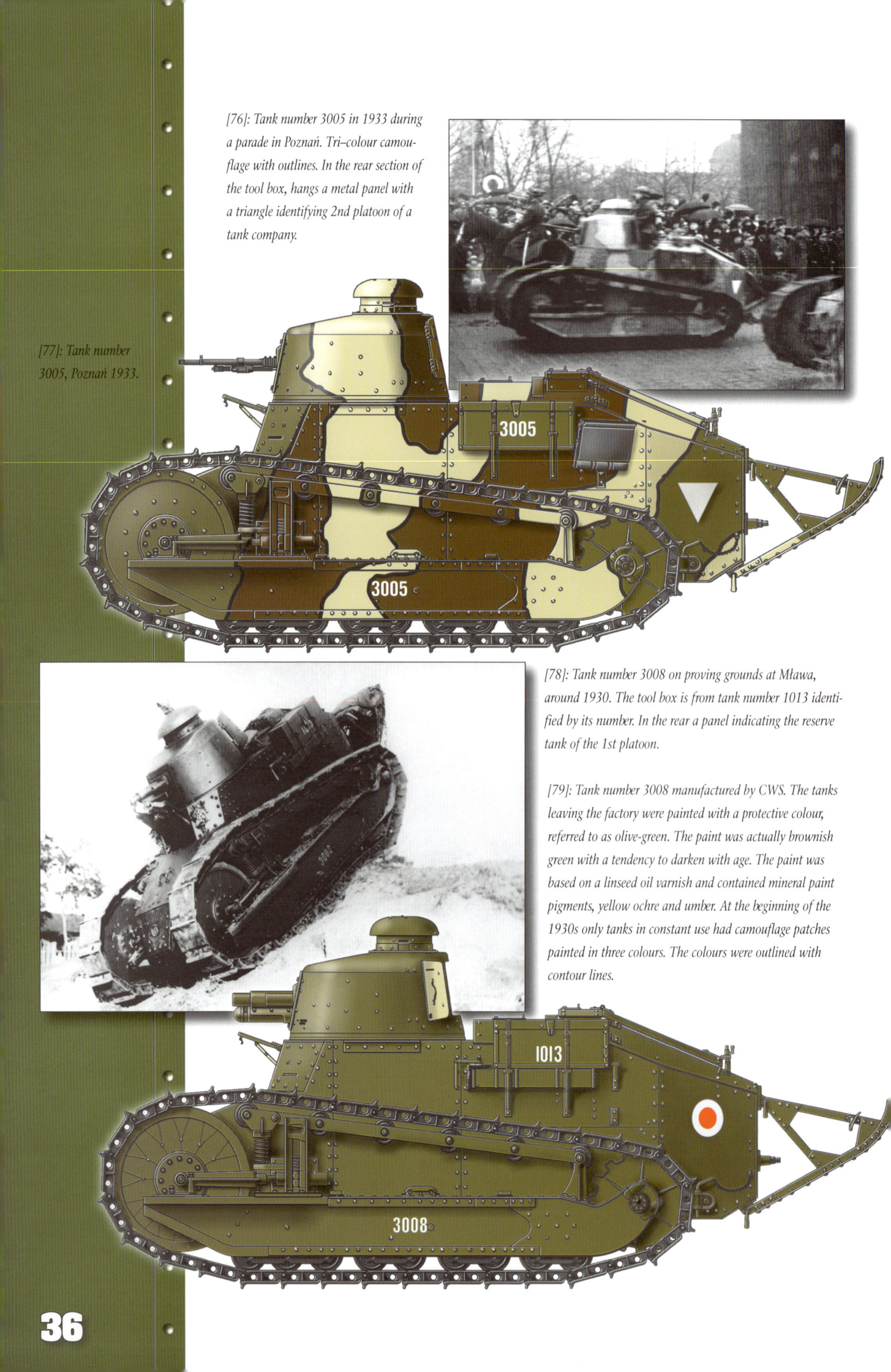

[76]: Tank number 3005 in 1933 during a parade in Poznań. Tri-colour camouflage with outlines. In the rear section of the tool box, hangs a metal panel with a triangle identifying 2nd platoon of a tank company.

[77]: Tank number 3005, Poznań 1933.

[78]: Tank number 3008 on proving grounds at Mława, around 1930. The tool box is from tank number 1013 identified by its number. In the rear a panel indicating the reserve tank of the 1st platoon.

[79]: Tank number 3008 manufactured by CWS. The tanks leaving the factory were painted with a protective colour, referred to as olive-green. The paint was actually brownish green with a tendency to darken with age. The paint was based on a linseed oil varnish and contained mineral paint pigments, yellow ochre and umber. At the beginning of the 1930s only tanks in constant use had camouflage patches painted in three colours. The colours were outlined with contour lines.

36

[80]: Tank number 3009 on Św. Marcin street in Poznań, 1933.

[81]: Tank number 3009 loaded onto Renault FU truck number 6939. The tank tank has camouflage in accordance with 1936 specifications.

[82]: Renault FU truck number 6939 and tank number 3009. The camouflage scheme dates to the first half of the 1930s.

[83]: Tank number 3010 on an obstacle course during an exhibition for aviation cadets.

[84]: Tank number 3012 during bridge crossing exercise in Modlin.

[85]: Tank number 3010. Parade at Poznań, 1933.

38

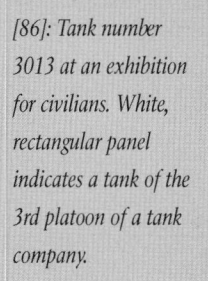

[86]: Tank number 3013 at an exhibition for civilians. White, rectangular panel indicates a tank of the 3rd platoon of a tank company.

[87]: Tank number 3014.

[88]: Tank number 3017. Headquarters drill in Rembertów.

[89]: Tank number 3023. An exhibition for aviation cadets.

[90]: Tank number 3027 left at Przemyśl.

[91]: The camouflage is in accordance with 1936 specifications, however still bearing the old registration number. It is possible that the tank did not have a new, 1939, registration number, or the old number was not over-painted. Note the front track tensioning wheel is of non standard design

40

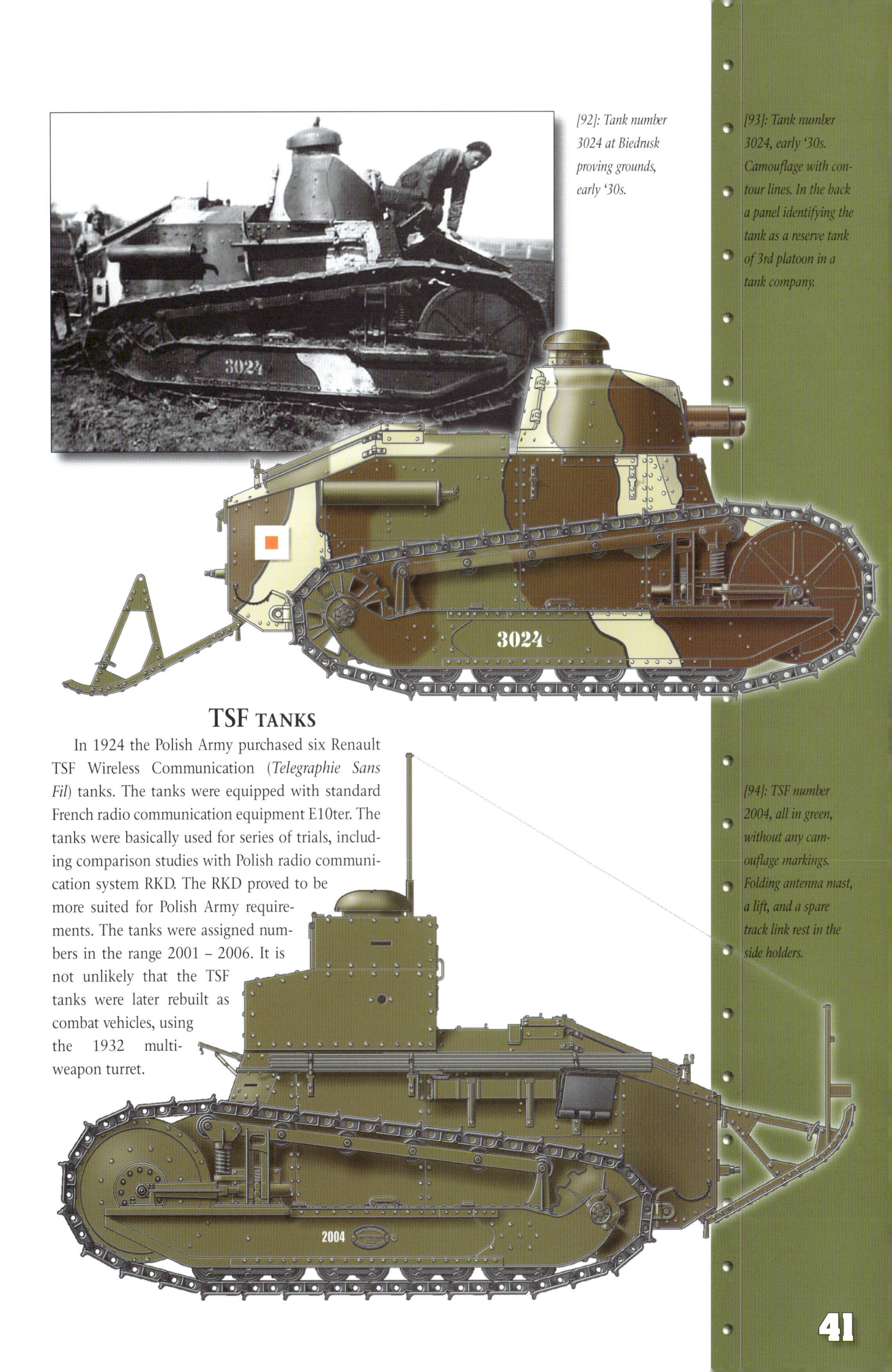

[92]: Tank number 3024 at Biedrusk proving grounds, early '30s.

[93]: Tank number 3024, early '30s. Camouflage with contour lines. In the back a panel identifying the tank as a reserve tank of 3rd platoon in a tank company.

TSF TANKS

In 1924 the Polish Army purchased six Renault TSF Wireless Communication (*Telegraphie Sans Fil*) tanks. The tanks were equipped with standard French radio communication equipment E10ter. The tanks were basically used for series of trials, including comparison studies with Polish radio communication system RKD. The RKD proved to be more suited for Polish Army requirements. The tanks were assigned numbers in the range 2001 – 2006. It is not unlikely that the TSF tanks were later rebuilt as combat vehicles, using the 1932 multi-weapon turret.

[94]: TSF number 2004, all in green, without any camouflage markings. Folding antenna mast, a lift, and a spare track link rest in the side holders.

41

[95]: Renault TSF number 2004. Photograph taken in 1930.

SMOKE SCREEN TANK

In 1926 one of the FT-17 tanks was rebuilt into a smoke screen tank. The original Polish nomenclature was not very fortunate, since the project was designated as a "gas tank" (*czołg gazowy*). Such a term misleadingly indicated chemical warfare equipment. The tank was tested until 1928. Eventually the project was abandoned, and the tank was most likely rebuilt back to its initial combat form.

[95]: Renault smoke screen tank towing an old German 85 mm anti-aircraft gun.

[97]: Proving ground exercise in 1927. On the left, a half tracked Citroen B2 10CV with press representatives.

[98]: Renault laying a smoke screen, photograph from May 1926 trials.

ARMOURED RAIL VEHICLES

After the war of 1920 Poland retained a total of 10 armoured trains in active duty, and as a mobilization reserve. The tactical principles of an armoured train operation required light, armoured rail vehicles (*drezyna pancerna*) to operate as scouts in conjunction with the armoured train. This type of vehicle was sometimes referred to as a drezine or draisine (*German*). The first of the two drezines assigned to each train was used for reconnaissance in front, while the second secured the rear of the train.

A number of Czechoslovakian armoured drezines Tatra was purchased. The vehicles did not quite meet the expectations. They were underpowered, which caused their acceleration to be very slow, and their track gradient negotiating ability poor.

[99]: The first prototype of the type R rail transporter. The mechanism was rather complex. The propulsion was obtained from tank's tracks revolving on the rollers underneath. The rollers mounted to the frame, and were an integral part of the transporter. The motion was further transmitted, through a set of gears, from the rollers to the front axle.

[100]: The R drezine in its final form.

[101]: The R drezine coupled with TK drezines. A characteristic bamboo radio-antenna mast may be noted.

An improved solution was a self propelled tank carrier (*drezyna pancerna torowo – terenowa*). It was a rail transporter designed to carry the FT-17 tank.

The transporter was propelled along the track by means of the tank's engine. A special extension mounted at the rear of the tank's gearbox allowed connection of an external shaft. The shaft, with Cardan joints, connected the engine to the rear axle of the transporter. In order to power the transporter, the side clutches of the tank had to be disengaged. The time necessary to drive the tank off the transporter, including uncoupling the shaft, was about 3 minutes. The reverse procedure took about 5 minutes. During transport the bottom of the tank rested on the frame of the transporter, and the tracks sat atop two pivoting beams. The beams, connected to a cross member of

[102]: Foreign military officials visiting 1st Armoured Train Troop (1 Dywizjon Pociągów Pancernych). In front, the TK rail transporter without the tankette, next the R drezine with FT-17 tank, The view of the second TK drezine is obstructed by the officers. In the background the exercise train of the 1st Troop - "Poznańczyk".

[103]: A complete TK-R-TK drezine unit seen from the rear.

[104]: The R drezine assigned to armoured train "Danuta". The tank and the transporter in the camouflage scheme introduced in 1936. New regulations regarding registration plates were implemented in the 1st Armoured Train Troop around 1939. The original number of the tank was over painted, and the registration plate was inside the tank. The registration plate of the transporter was fixed to the front beam of the frame.

45

[105]: The front and rear view of one of the first R rail transporters. Atop the transporter sits a Polish made CWS tank.

the frame, could be hoisted to horizontal position. This allowed for clearance between the tank's hull and the transporter's frame, necessary for manoeuvring of the tank. The beams were operated by means of a hydraulic lift, also mounted to the frame. The frame of the transporter was welded from angular steel beams and sheet metal. Two exit ramp extensions at the end were spring loaded. The leaf springs kept them at a set height above the rail, at the same time allowing for the downward collapse under the weight of the tank. The transporter had two railroad wheel sets with helical springs. At the end opposite to the ramp, two regulation railroad buffers and a coupling were mounted. The transporter, also referred to as drezine R (*drezyna R*), had the ability to pull about 25 tonnes. This allowed for creation of a set of drezines called TK-R-TK. The TK rail transporter was designed for the TK-3 and TKS tankettes. Two TK transporters were coupled with a single FT-17 transporter used to power the train.

In action of the TK-R-TK drezines, the FT-17 tank could be used in the field. However it typically remained on the transporter, providing artillery support for the machine gun armed tankettes.

[106]: A complete TK-R-TK reconnaissance rail transporter system operated by the 1st Armoured Train Troop.

Attempts to modernise FT-17 tanks

The possibilities for modifying the FT-17 tank were considered as early as the first years of the Polish-Soviet War. Military operations had shown a number of shortcomings, particularly high fuel consumption and low speed.

In April of 1921, Captain Kardaszewicz developed a track in which the modular chain links were joined together without the use of hinges and pins. The design was not quite successful and was never taken past the trial stage. But it had shown that the improvement in mobility of the tank could be achieved by changing its traction system. The speed of the tank rose to 12 km/h, and the fuel consumption dropped.

In 1924 a new track was created. It could be best described as a narrow link track. The speed of the tank increased only slightly, however the vibrations were reduced and the fuel efficiency was greatly improved. A modified version of the narrow link track went into production; enough sets were made to retrofit 65 tanks.

In 1926 one of the standard tanks was extensively rebuilt. This prototype became known as type "M". Cooling, exhaust, and fuel systems were changed. An enlarged gas tank was installed. A number of significant changes in armour were also introduced. The trials were successful, however due to the high cost of modifications the plan was not carried out. A few attempts to improve the armament were also undertaken. A new turret, housing a 37 mm cannon and a machine gun, was constructed in 1929. After testing at the Armoured - Motorized Experimental Group (*Doświadczalna Grupa Pancerno-Motorowa*), the turret was declared as unacceptable. At first, the turret was mounted on FT-17, next on M 26/27 tank. Another multi-weapon turret, armed with 37 mm cannon and the wz.30 Browning heavy machine gun, was

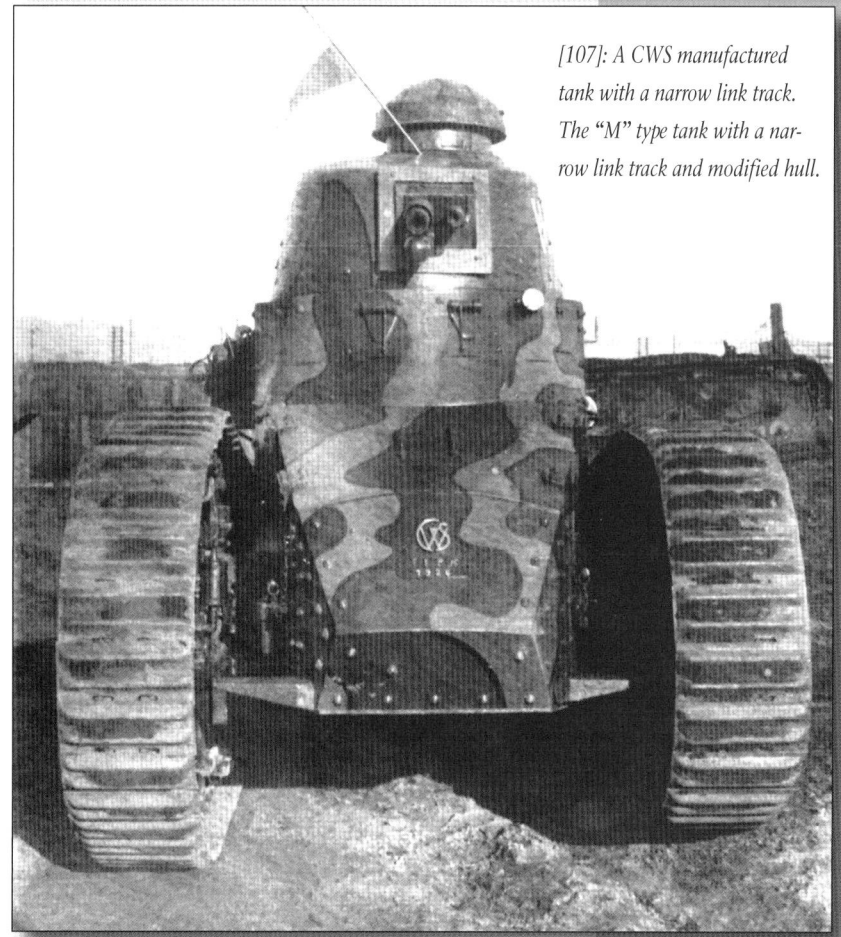

[107]: A CWS manufactured tank with a narrow link track. The "M" type tank with a narrow link track and modified hull.

constructed in 1932. It was not accepted for production, although there is a possibility that six such turrets were constructed and used. This project was abandoned because at the time all further attempts to modify Renault FT-17 tank were suspended. The tank was declared obsolete and unworthy of any modernization. The work on replacing the original Renault traction system with one based on a Vickers design was suspended for the same reason. The Renault / Vickers tank, designated Renault wz.32, equipped with 37 mm cannon and a machine gun, was capable of 13 km/h. This speed was not considered to be satisfactory.

[108]: Renault type "M" named "Hanuś". The two-tone camouflage with contour lines is non-standard and unique.

[109]: Tank "M" at Biedrusk proving grounds (enlarged fragment of the photograph from page 19).

M 26/27 tanks

As time went on it become obvious to Polish military officials that the Renault FT-17 was becoming obsolete. Some considerations were made as to the replacement of the FT-17 with the M 26/27, also known as NC-2. The French were also aware of the FT-17's shortcomings. The M 26/27 tank, fitted with the Kegresse rubber track and suspension, was tested as one of the solutions. Five M 26/27 tanks were purchased, but their performance was found to be nearly equivalent to their predecessor, so no further steps were taken. One of the tanks, designated Renault wz.29, was used for trials with a multi-weapon turret.

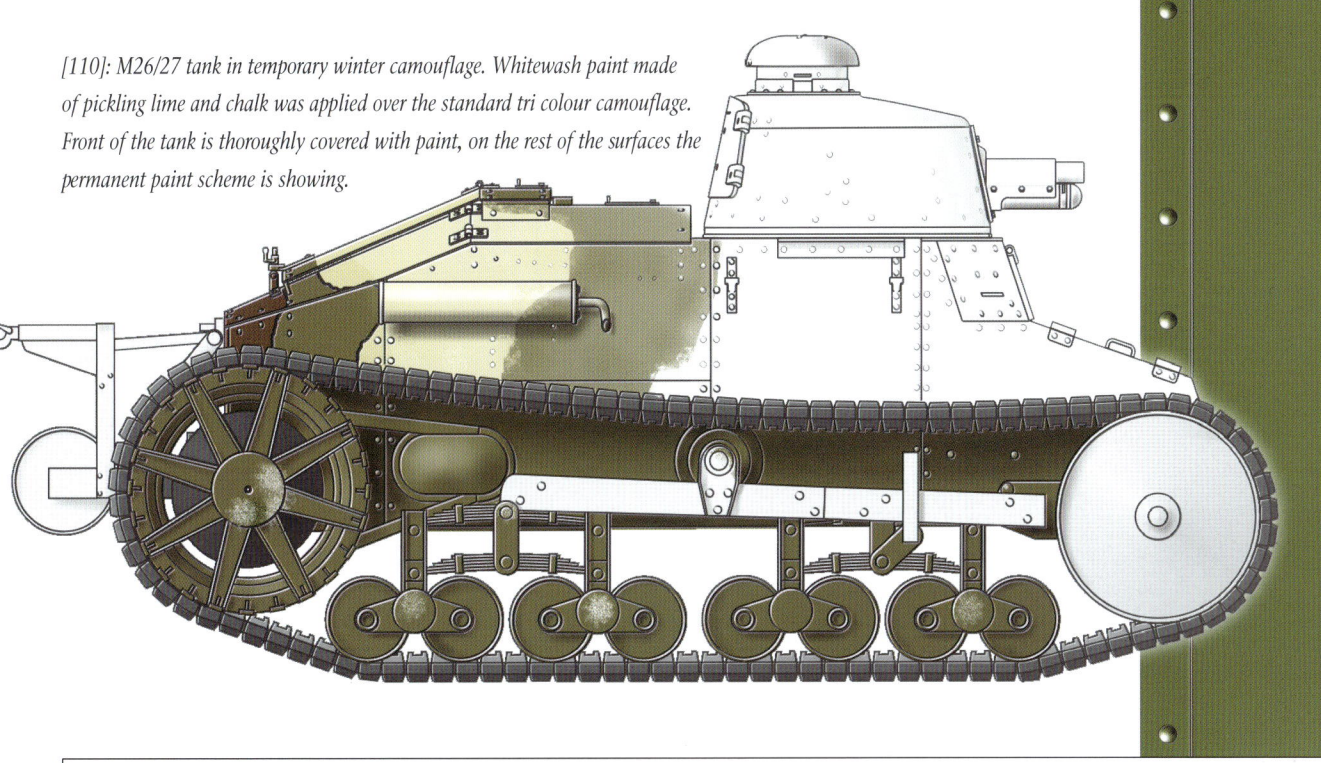

[110]: M26/27 tank in temporary winter camouflage. Whitewash paint made of pickling lime and chalk was applied over the standard tri colour camouflage. Front of the tank is thoroughly covered with paint, on the rest of the surfaces the permanent paint scheme is showing.

[111]: M26/27 tank during field exercise.

[112]: M26/27 tanks during winter exercise.

[113]: M26/27 tank on a pontoon bridge. The tank has a multi-weapon turret mounted for trials.

NC1 tank

Only one NC1, according to other nomenclature NC27, tank was imported from France. This model was yet another attempt to improve the FT-17. It had modified armour and a completely different suspension system, with characteristic vertically positioned helical springs. The NC1 model was found not much superior to its predecessor. As a result the NC1, numbered 1153, was the only tank of this type used in Poland. There are documents with a mention of a purchase of 24 tanks of this type. There is however, no known documentation related to the service of these tanks with the Polish armed forces, nor photographs depicting the NC27 tank, other than 1153.

[114]: NC1 tank on Renault FU lorry, registration number 6936.

[115]: A view of the NC1 tank from the front and side. The tank is painted in the regulation brownish green paint. Front and side numbers are in different fonts.

[116]: NC1 tank number 1153.

52

September of 1939

Renault FT-17 in September campaign of 1939

On 6 September 1939 the 2nd Armoured Battalion mobilized three independent tank companies equipped with Renault FT-17 tanks. The 111th, 112th, and 113th Companies were under the control of the Commander in Chief (*Naczelny Wódz*) as support units.

The 111th Company was transported via rail from Przemyśl to Siedlce. On 9 September the transport was bombed near Łuków Podlaski. The company was unloaded, and directed to the nearby forest due to the very limited amount of fuel. The outpost tanks engaged advancing German armoured unit; two Renault tanks were lost as a result. Polish retreat from the area forced the

[117]: FT-17 tank number 1024 on the road.

[118]: Another photograph of tank 1024.

[119]: FT-17 tank in Grudziądz. This poor quality photograph is rather significant, it illustrates one of the very few tanks used in units other than the 2nd Armoured Battalion in Żurawica and armoured train regiments. One or two tanks were at Cavalry Training Centre (Centrum Wyszkolenia Kawalerii) in Grudziądz. At least two more tanks, numbered 3018 and 3025, at Modlin fortress. The tank 3025 was immobilized as part of the exhibition displaying retired armoured vehicles and artillery pieces. Both Modlin tanks had a 1936 camouflage painting.

[120]: FT-17 tank number 1126 on the road.

[121]: Unidentified Polish FT-17 tank captured by the Germans.

[122]: FT-17 tank as an entrenched pill box at Brześć fortress.

[123]: Tank number 1129, Brześć.

[124]: Another photograph of tank 1024. The white cross German insignia was typical on captured tanks.

[125]: FT-17 tank, number unknown, Brześć fortress.

[126]: One of the few FT-17 tanks painted according to the 1936 camouflage specifications. The number of the tank is not visible. It is very likely that the tank already had a new registration number. From 1938 a new registration method was implemented and registration plates were issued. Combat vehicles carried their plates inside.

57

[127]: Tank number 1038 with damaged track. This tank was assigned to the armoured train "Bartosz Głowacki". The tank was destroyed at the railroad crossing near Żabinka. The second tank of the drezine detachment and the tankettes were involved in the encounter with German armoured cars. All were destroyed a few hundred meters away. The crews survived and returned to the train.

[128]: Renault FT-17 tank number 1079. It seems that the tank still has a pre 1936 camouflage with contour lines.

[129]: Tank number 1097, abandoned in the gardens near Brześć. Old type of camouflage with vertical patches outlined by thin contour lines.

[130]: One of the R rail transporters, from an unidentified armoured train.

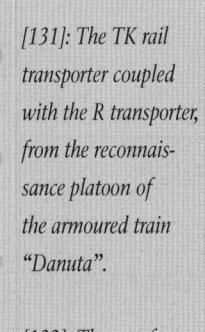

[131]: The TK rail transporter coupled with the R transporter, from the reconnaissance platoon of the armoured train "Danuta".

[132]: The set of TK-R-TK drezines used by armoured train "Poznańczyk".

[133]: Tank abandoned near Łowicz. It is probably the tank serving with armoured train "Piłsudczyk". On the side of the tank there is a German warning, written in chalk, forbidding removal of parts.

[134]: Renault FT-17 blocking the Lithuanian Gate (Brama Litewska) in Brześć fortress. Tank number 1102, partially burned, has early 1930s camouflage. The second tank, number 1071, has post-1936 camouflage.

[135]: Series of photographs of the damaged tank number 1142.

company to march south towards Radzymin where the fuel supply was exhausted and the tanks were destroyed by their own crews.

The 112th Company was also dispatched to Siedlce. The damage to the railroad line near Łuków forced a detour, sending the company to Brześć nad Bugiem. The tanks were absorbed into the defence system of the Brześć fortress. The tanks defended the approach to the main gate as stationary, trenched in, bunkers.

[136]: Series of photographs of the damaged tank number 1142.

[137]: The 1141 tank, disabled in the gardens outside the Brześć fortress.

The defenders abandoned the Brześć citadel on 16 September. The tanks attempted to break through the enemy lines, but the effort failed. Some of the crews were able to join the other formations.

The 113th Company railroad transport delayed near Łuków, was also re-routed to Brześć.

The company was employed patrolling the terrain on the perimeter of the fortress. On the day of most intense fighting, 14 September, almost all the tanks were lost in action.

After the fall of Brześć some of the crews joined the Independent Operational Group "Polesie" (*Samodzielna Grupa Operacyjna "Polesie"*).

An improvised armoured unit, created from the exercise and training tanks left behind in Żurawica, also participated in fighting. It defended the town of Przemyśl.

[138]: One more photograph of tank number 1141, taken at an earlier time. The machine gun is still in place and a protective tarp may be visible. The tarp was most likely used to mask the tank.

12th Armoured Battalion

The 12th Armoured Battalion was created on 26 April 1937 in Łuck. Just like all other armoured regiments at that time, this was an independent unit responsible for its own logistics, training, personnel, and equipment maintenance.

In 1938 Poland bought one Renault R35 tank (according to other sources, two or three such tanks). Inability to increase production of the Polish 7TP tank led to the necessity of purchases abroad. France was an only option, partially for financial reasons. The most desirable tank was the Somua S35. However the French, well aware of the fact that this is their best tank, were rapidly rearming their own regiments with Somua S35. The only tank available for purchase was the Renault R35. The engines of these tanks had a tendency to overheat, the suspension was too stiff, and the cannon was rather obsolete. Nonetheless, the short 37 mm Puteaux cannon could be replaced with a longer, much better performing model. But even a slightly better, long barrel mod.18 S.A. was not available, so the Polish request could not be fulfilled. The French military doctrine of the time, did not envision using the tank force in an offensive manner. Renault R35 was an infantry support tank, and as such its speed of 19km/h on the road and 13km/h in the field was considered acceptable. Finally, the prolonged efforts to acquire new tanks succeeded. In April of 1939 100 tanks were bought. According to French standards it was two complete battalions with spare tanks. Three additional Hotchkiss H35 tanks were acquired for comparison studies.

The first half of the order was fulfilled at the beginning of July 1939, and 49 tanks were send via rail to 12th Armoured Battalion at Łuck. This transport also included the mechanical shop and support vehicles - Renault and Latil, five all terrain Laffly vehicles, as well as full assortment of spare parts, ammunition for the cannons and machine guns.

This equipment was initially staged at the French 505th Tank Regiment prior to shipment to Poland. Some tanks were brand new; some came from French Army reserves. All the latter tanks had very low, or even negligible mileage, but a lot of cannons came from the old FT-17 tanks rearmed with machine guns. Some cannons had corrosion pits inside the barrels.

It was possible to establish only some of the numbers assigned to Polish tanks. The numbers and the respective fate are as follows:

50903 – detained in Romania; 50912 – Romania; 50918 – Romania; 50920 – Romania;

50921 – Romania; 50924 – Romania; 50925 – Romania; 50927 – Romania; 50928 – Romania; 50929 – Romania; 50933 – Romania; 50934 – Romania; 50943 – Romania;

50947 – detained in Hungary; 50948 – Romania; 50955 - Romania; 50956 – Romania; 50961 – Romania; 50962 – Romania; 50964 – Romania; 50971 –Hungary; 50976 – Romania; 50984 – purchased in 1938, Romania; 50987 – Romania; 50989 – Romania; 50990 – Romania; 50995; 50998

[139]: Renault R35 tank number 50984. The tank was purchased for trials.

[140]: Renault R35 number 50984 - front, rear view.

– Romania; 51000 – Romania; 51003 – Romania; 51004 – Hungary; 51005 – Romania; 51007 – Romania; 51008 – Romania; 51009 – captured by USSR; 51011 – Romania; 51017 – Romania; 51022 – Romania.

The numbers of Hotchkiss H35 tanks remain unknown.

21st Light Tank Battalion

During the September mobilization the 12th Armoured Battalion fielded the 21st Light Tank Battalion. The battalion had 45, or 46, Renault R35 tanks. The tanks were organized in three combat companies. Each company had four platoons with tanks and a company commander tank. An additional six reserve tanks were in the support and repair company.

On 3 September, the 21st Battalion left the garrison and dispersed in the nearby woods and orchards. On September 12 the tanks were ordered to the railway stations in Łuck and Kiwerce. The anticipated transport was not available due to the lack of appropriate railway wagons. On 14 of September the tanks were directed towards Dubno, and then loaded on a train. The train departed towards Żółkiew with the intention of delivering the battalion to the 10th Cavalry Brigade. The railroad track destruction forced the tanks to unload at Radziwiłłów. The battalion

[141]: Renault R35 tanks in Hungary; tank number 51004.

[142]: Tank number 50971 after crossing the Hungarian border.

had never reached the 10th Motorized Cavalry Brigade under Colonel Maczek. New orders from the Commander in Chief dispatched the battalion towards Stanisławów, with the intention of setting up a defence along Romanian border (*rumuńskie przedmoście*). The tanks regrouped on 16 September near Brzeżany. From Brzeżany the battalion moved to Stanisławów. On 17 September the battalion set up an encampment at Klubowce. The reserve tanks were ordered to secure the Dniestr River bridges in Niżniów; later they were to rejoin the unit. The concept of defensive perimeter along the Romanian border was abandoned on 17 September due to the Soviet invasion. The 21st Battalion was ordered to cross the Romanian border in Kuty. The order was carried out on 18 September. Two tanks were left in Kuty to cover other retreating units. Eventually these two tanks rejoined the battalion.

The reserve tanks, on the way back to the battalion, passed through Kołomyja where they were involved in an exchange of fire with Ukrainian militia. The militiamen decorated the buildings with red flags in anticipation of the Red Army arrival.

[143]: Photograph showing the damage to the control arm of the first road wheel of tank 50971.

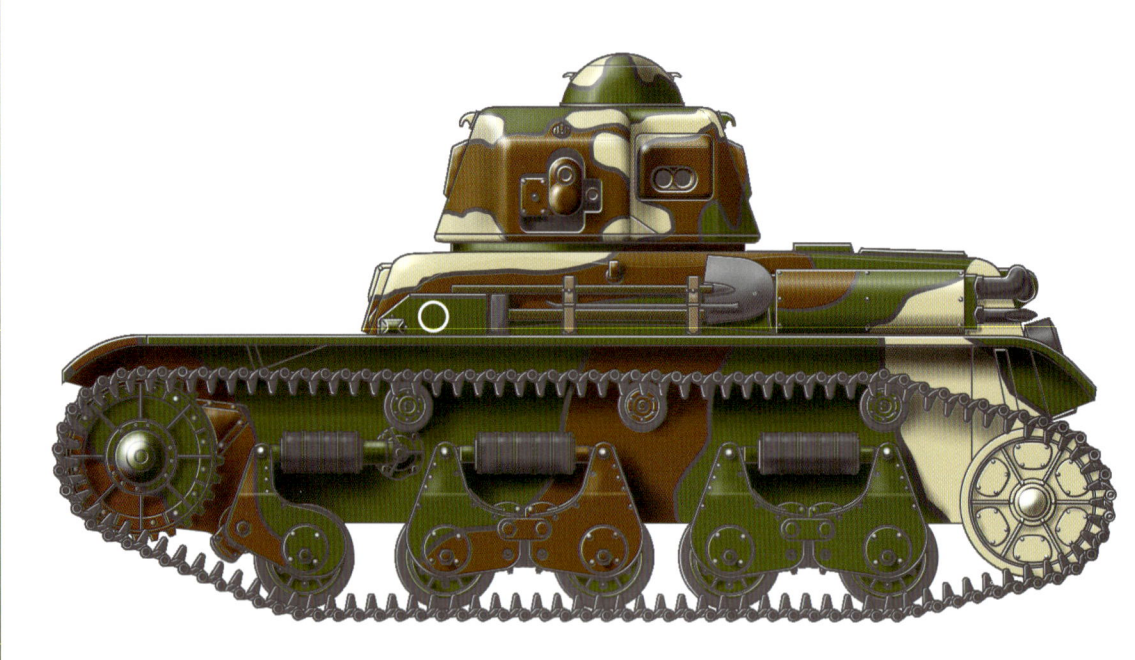

[144]: Tank 50947, with tri-colour camouflage and contour lines painted according to French standards. The white circle is left over from the tank's service in France. The emblem indicated a tank of the 1st company. It was never painted over during its short service with the Polish army.

[145]: Renault R35 tanks in Hungary; tank number 50947 next to the tank number 50971.

[146]: Example of false propaganda, tank number 50947, with red star. Presented as captured Soviet tank during the war trophy exhibition.

68

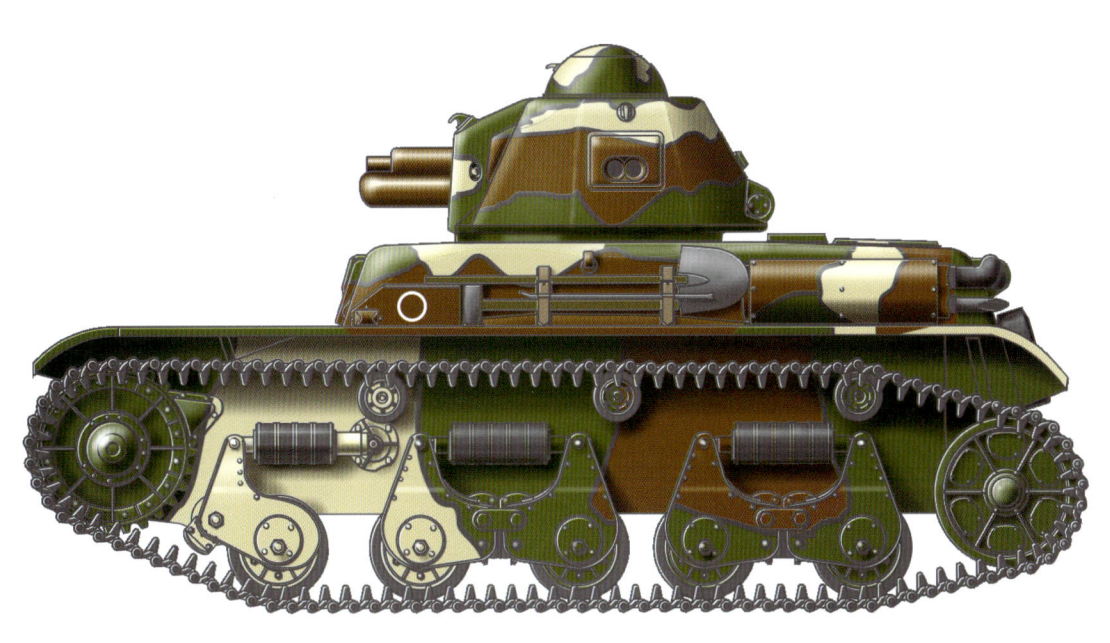

[147]: Tank 50104, with tri-colour camouflage and contour lines painted according to French standards. The white circle is left over from the tank's service in France.

[148]: Rear view of the tank number 50947.

[149]: Tank number 50971 after repair.

69

Half company of Lieutenant Jakubowicz

After the departure of the 21st Battalion, the Łuck garrison continued the organization of crews for the second delivery of the Renault R35 tanks. After 11 September it become obvious that the delivery will not materialize in time. The standing order of departure to deliver the tanks from Romanian ports was cancelled.

Around 14 September Lieutenant Jakubowicz organized his unit into a combat one, equivalent to half a company. The unit was equipped with tanks left behind after the departure of the 21st Battalion, and equipment evacuated from the Main Armoured Unit Armoury (*Główna Składnica Broni Pancernych*). There were four Renault R35 left at the garrison, three Hotchkiss H35 tanks were obtained from the Kiwerce railroad station. One of the R35 tanks was severely damaged due to an accident during accelerated crew training. The attempts to repair the tank failed, so it was blown up prior to departure.

On September 17 Lieutenant Jakubowicz's unit departed towards Łuck as a rear guard of the General Skuratowicz group. As the road towards the Romanian frontier was cut off by the advance of the Red Army, the destination was changed to Lwów. On 19 September near Busko, one of the tanks experienced a mechanical failure. Soon after, a Red Army unit approached. In the encounter, one tank and its crew were lost. Another mechanical breakdown occurred outside of Busko, the tank had to be blown up. Near the town of Krasne the remaining tanks exchanged fire with Ukrainian militia or communist diversion group.

On 20 September the tanks had an encounter with Germans near Kamionka Strumiłowa. One tank was lost in this otherwise successful battle.

On 22 September the unit, with only two tanks and a few automobiles left, joined the 12th Heavy Artillery Regiment (*12 Dywizjon Artylerii Najcięższej*). The news of the capitulation of Lwów forced a change of direction towards Bełz. Near Dołchobyczów the column had to break away from Soviet infantry supported by tanks. During this manoeuvre one of the R35 was damaged damaged. The tank was set on fire and abandoned. Next day, or possibly on 24 September, the last tank was set ablaze due to lack of fuel and spare parts.

[150]: Another view of tank number 50971.

[151]: Tank number 51004 in Hungary.

[152]: Tank number 51004 in Hungary.

71

[153]: Tank number 51009 fell into Soviet hands. It was repaired with parts obtained from other damaged R35 tanks. The tank was subjected to extensive trials.

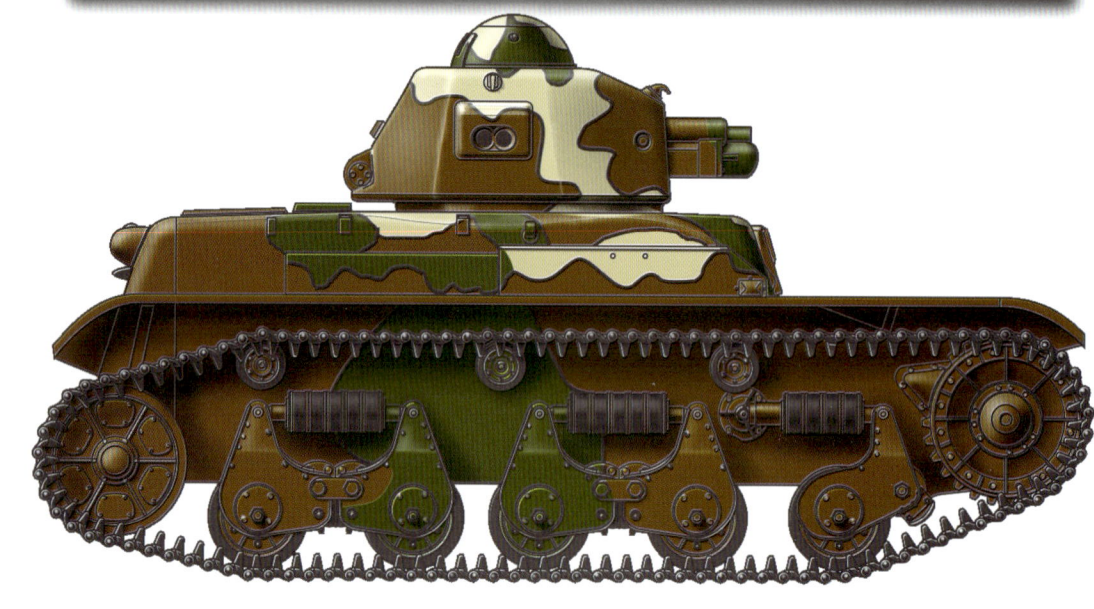

Soldiers and tanks of General Maczek

In the afternoon of 19 September 1939 the 10th Mechanized Cavalry Brigade (*10 Brygada Kawalerii Zmotoryzowanej*) crossed the Polish – Hungarian border. The brigade had all the cannons, anti-aircraft guns, and mortars that were issued during mobilization on 1 September. The only anti-tank guns that were missing were destroyed by enemy fire or tanks. The brigade led a fair number of German prisoners of war, along with captured equipment. Colonel Maczek's 10th Brigade was crossing the border as a result of a direct order. The troops were not fleeing, they were retreating to regroup, and continue the fight for Poland.

Coëtquidan

The military camp at Coëtquidan was where the Polish Army was recreated. Coëtquidan is located in Brittany, in the department of Morbihan, 45 kilometres from Rennes. Polish headquarters were established there at the end of September 1939. First groups of volunteers begun to arrive almost at the same time. The volunteers came from Polish families who migrated to France and Belgium in search of employment between the wars. A total of 44,700 men from France, Belgium, and Holland joined the newly forming Polish Army in exile. Parallel to the draft in France, evacuation of army personnel detained in Hungary and Romania after the September Campaign was initiated. Some 34,000 soldiers were able to escape the internment camps. Additional 4,000 men came from Syria.

At the end of October 1939 Stanisław Maczek was nominated as commanding officer of the camp. General Sikorski promoted Colonel Maczek to the rank of brigadier general (*generał brygady*) for the valour and fortitude displayed during the Polish Campaign of 1939. The French strongly insisted on creation of as many infantry units as possible. Polish officers, after the experiences of the September Campaign, realized the need for armoured and motorized units. General Maczek was determined to create a light mechanized division against all odds.

The first step towards the achievement of this goal was an appropriate segregation of army personnel.

Soldiers of cavalry and armoured unit were separated from the rest. They were transferred to the newly created Cavalry Group *(Zgrupowanie Kawalerii)* at Paimpont, and Armoured Group (*Zgrupowanie Broni Pancernej*) at Campénéac, both near Coëtquidan. On the 2 of December the 1st Tank Battalion (*1 Batalion Czołgów*) was created at camp Campénéac. The conditions were difficult. There were shortages of uniforms, blankets, heating fuel and most importantly, weapons. The help extended by Lieutenant Colonel Loisel, French liaison officer, was invaluable. This old,

[154]: Emblem of 10th Mechanized Cavalry Brigade in France 1940.

[155]: Polish Renault tanks on the obstacle course at St. Cécile les Vignes.

one armed, veteran of the First World War used to say that the Polish tank battalion was his last love. On January 29 1940 the 2nd Tank Battalion was formed from the spare resources of the 1st Battalion. The Cavalry Group formed three battalions. The uhlans battalion *(batalion ułanów)* later evolved into the 24th Uhlans Regiment (*24 Pułk Ułanów*). The mounted rifles battalion (*batalion strzelców konnych*) later evolved into the 10th Mounted Rifles Regiment (*10 Pułk Strzelców Konnych*) and the training battalion. Both regiments fought in the September Campaign as part of the 10th Mechanized Cavalry Brigade. Both were able to save their regimental banners and bring them from Hungary to France.

[156]: *The emblem over the entry gate to the Polish camp at Coëtquidan.*

[157]: *Dragoon battalion during an exercise march on the road near Burie. Officers may be noted, among them Major Emil Słatyński battalion commander, commander of the heavy machine gun squadron Captain (rotmistrz) Jan Maciejowski, and Lieutenant Jan Salwa holding a map.*

In the Rodan valley

In the first days of February a decision was made to create an armoured and motorized units camp near Orange in the Avignon region. Both groups were transported by rail to their new locations. The 1st and the 2nd Tank Battalions, along with origins of the 3rd and the 4th Battalions, as well as the Armoured Training Centre (*Centrum Wyszkolenia Broni Pancernej*) were placed at Sainte-Cécile-les-Vignes, Cairanne and Piolenc. The 24th Uhlans Regiment and the 10th Mounted Rifles Regiment were at Mornas. The training battalion and camp headquarters were stationed in Bollène.

The training of the cavalry formations was seriously impeded, if not impossible, due to lack of any equipment. The Cavalry Group was to field squadrons of motorcycles, machine guns, mortars and anti-tank artillery. The only available weaponry was a limited amount of rifles. The other necessary training equipment was never sent to Orange.

The situation of the Armoured Group was better. The 1st Tank Battalion received ten FT-17 tanks. The 2nd Battalion, in the final phases of formation, also had ten FT-17. Incomplete 3rd and

[158]: **Above left:** The 10th Dragoons Regiment of the Brigade. Motorcycles with sidecars were brand new Indian 741 obtained from the American arms and supply shipment for the French army. Motorcycle in the background was most likely a Peugeot 107.

[159]: **Above:** The dragoons and their motorcycles. Indian 741 motorcycle, behind it, one of the Peugeot 350 ccm. On the Indian motorcycle, cadet (aspirant) Stefan Bałuk, in the sidecar cadet A. Krzyczkowski.

[160]: **Left:** March 16 1940. Unloading of tanks at Orange railroad station.

4th Battalions were assigned a few tanks each. Some time later, initial steps were taken to create the 5th, 6th Tank Battalions and a Reserve Battalion at Piolenc.

In the middle of February 1940 a volunteer draft was announced for an independent tank company. The company was created as a support to the Highlander Brigade (*Brygada Strzelców Podhalańskich*). Both units were to become a part of an expeditionary corps dispatched to aid Finland in the conflict with the USSR. The company was formed, equipped, and ready for departure in record-breaking time. A few Renault FT-17 and two Hotchkiss H39 tanks were used as training equipment. As the expedition plans were abandoned, the company never received the combat equipment. At the beginning of May the unit was transferred south to Lagarde-Paréol, few kilometres away from St. Cecile. At the end of May, the company was incorporated into the 1st Tank Battalion.

In April 1940 one more training group was established in order to compliment the planned mechanized division. The Motorised Artillery Group (*Zgrupowanie Artylerii Motorowej*) was created in Lapalud.

[161]: Renault tanks on the exercise field at St. Cécile les Vignes, first to the left was numbered 69651.

[162]: Renault tanks on the exercise field at St. Cécile les Vignes.

[163]: Renault tanks on the exercise field at St. Cecile les Vignes. Among the officers are commander of the 1st Battalion Major Leonard Furs-Żyrkiewicz, and company commander Captain Iwanowski. Quality of the photograph makes it impossible to see the details of an interesting pain scheme of the tank.

[164]: Renault tanks on the exercise field at St. Cécile les Vignes.

[165]: Tank number 69651. The number partially blurred, the last two digits were repainted using a larger stencil. Tri colour camouflage with contour lines.

[166]: Tank number 69651.

77

[167]: Renault tanks at Cécile les Vignes, the first one is numbered 61651.

[168]: Soldiers posing with a tank at St. Cécile les Vignes, the number of the tank in not recognisable.

[169]: Renault tanks on the exercise field at St. Cécile les Vignes, during crew briefing.

[170]: Officers posing with a tank at St. Cécile les Vignes.

[171]: St.Cécile les Vignes. First tank to the left has a number 69651.

[172]: Crews and their tanks. First tank to the left has a number 69651. St.Cécile les Vignes.

[173]: Renault tanks on the exercise field at St. Cécile les Vignes, the numbers remain unknown.

[174]: Tank number 69651.

[175]: Renault tanks on the exercise field at St. Cécile les Vignes.

[176]: Tanks at the shooting ground at Lagarde-Paréol.

[177]: Tank number 67592 at St. Cécile les Vignes.

[178]: Tank attack exercise at St. Cécile les Vignes.

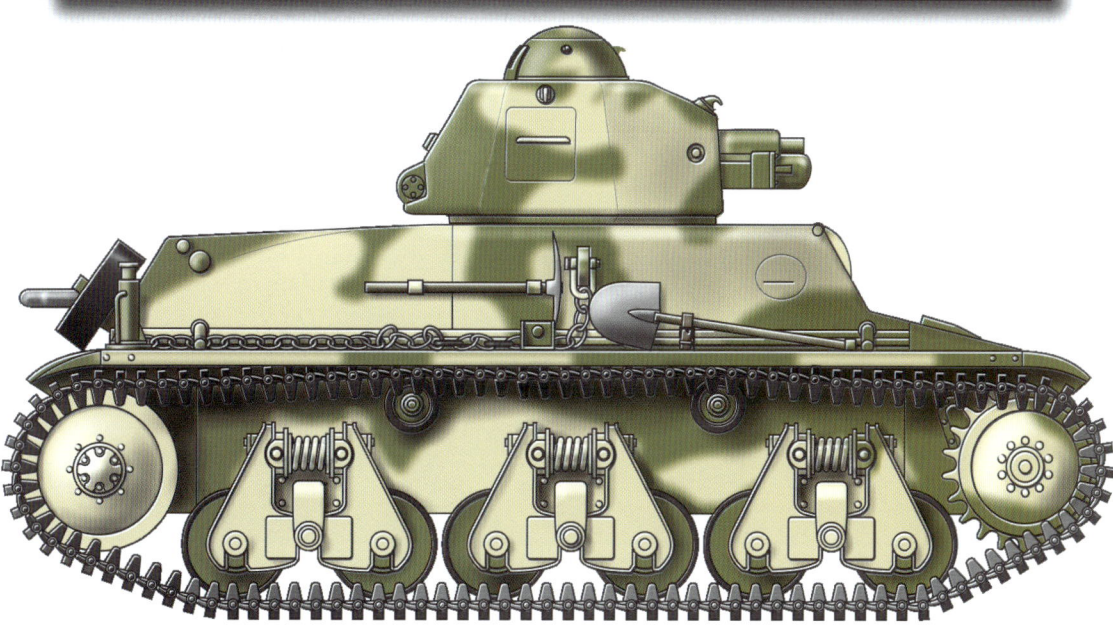

[179]: Tank number 70210 from the Finnish Company. Only some of the patches of the tri-colour camouflage have black outlines. The tank number is painted on the tail, the number on the suspension beam is overpainted. The tank has no armament.

[180]: Tank number 70210 from the Finnish Company on a lift. One of the road wheel bogies is being repaired. In the background, a tank with number unknown and a tank with number ending in ...551.

[181]: Hotchkiss H39 number 40755 belonging to Finnish Company. Two tone camouflage with patches applied through a spray gun.

81

[182]: Finnish Company volunteers and their tanks.

[183]: Four Finnish Company tanks.

[184]: Finnish Company tank crews alongside one of their tanks.

[185]: Both Hotchkiss tanks of the Finnish Company.

[186]: Finnish Company tank crewmen with Hotchkiss H39 number 40755.

[187]: Hotchkiss H39 number 40755.

83

[188]: Hotchkiss number 40755. Captain Kazimierz Martini is the officer visible in all photographs. He was a technical officer of the Finnish Company.

[189]: The second Hotchkiss tank of the Finnish Company. On the right, front part of Hotchkiss 40755 may be noted.

[190]: The second Hotchkiss tank of the Finnish Company with unidentified number. Two tone painting, dark brown patches sprayed over the dark green- brown background.

Near Paris

On 10 May 1940 the German offensive begun. Rapid advances of the enemy made the matter of arming the Polish units urgent. But only at the Polish camp, the French authorities remained indifferent. Until 21 May nothing happened, with the exception on an order to form anti-commando units to defend the area against German paratroopers. This order was issued by the French region commander (*major de zône*). On 21 May a French-Polish Mission (*Misja Francusko-Polska*) liaison officer had arrived with orders. The orders called for an immediate formation and dispatch of six anti-tank artillery squadrons the very same day. Next day the orders were retracted, and a decision to form a light mechanized division was announced. But there was no time to complete this task.

On 24 May General Maczek begun an urgent formation of a motorized armour brigade. The brigade was to consist of the following units: a command; a two battalion tank regiment, 45 tanks in each battalion; a two battalion motorized cavalry regiment; an artillery troop with two 105 mm batteries; an anti-tank artillery troop with two 25 mm batteries and two 47 mm batteries; a 25 mm anti - aircraft battery; a communication squadron; a pioneer company and support units.

The pace was insane. On May 25, 300 drivers had to be dispatched to collect vehicles of all categories. On 27 May the 1st Tank Regiment, with its 1st and 2nd Tank Battalions, was transported by rail towards Paris. On 29 May the cavalry departed to the same location. Next day all other units followed. The 3rd, 4th, 5th and 6th Tank Battalion, the Reserve Battalion and the Training Centre remained in Orange.

The brigade's headquarters, communication squadron, and traffic control platoon were stationed in château Corbeville and town of Orsay. The cavalry regiment in Arpajon, and the tank regiment in Camp de Satory near Versailles.

In a few days, all the months wasted in the winter had to be made up for. Additional reinforcements had arrived, such as an infantry battalion from Coëtquidan, which had to be reassigned to cavalry squadrons. A 25 mm anti-tank artillery company, a 47 mm anti-tank artillery battery, a 25 mm anti-aircraft batteries had to be merged into artillery units. A group of about 200 air-force personnel had to be assigned as drivers and technical specialists.

At the same time the equipment was flowing in. Tanks, trucks, motorcycles, armament, ammunition, uniforms, field kitchens etc. All this brand new, from factories or military depots. However, the soldiers were for the most part not familiar with this equipment. The entire winter was spent on exercises, in which the tanks and cannons were simulated by signal flags.

[191]: Renault R35 tank during an exercise drive. In the turret Master Corporal/Cadet (plutonowy podchorąży) Brzozowski.

[192]: The column of the 10th Brigade vehicles at rest on a road through the woods. In front, a half tracked Unic TU1 with ammunition trailer. Behind it, small Peugeot DK5 J trucks.

10TH CAVALRY BRIGADE

The 1st Tank Battalion obtained Renault R35, R35 modifié 39, and Renault R40 tanks. A few training drives and a shooting practice were conducted. The 2nd Battalion was still waiting to be equipped when the Brigade received an ultimatum. It was demanded that the Brigade immediately dispatches all the units that are in readiness. If this demand could not be fulfilled, all the so far received equipment was to be returned. This armament could, supposedly, be supplied to other French units waiting to be equipped.

Polish High Command intended to have this decision arbitrated by General Weygand.

One additional week was needed for the Brigade to achieve full battle readiness. General Sikorski, Commander in Chief of the Polish Armed Forces (*Naczelny Wódz*), was formulating his reply, while General Weygand telephoned Polish headquarters. In his statement General Weygand announced that every single bayonet and tank are critical at this very moment.

Furthermore, General Weygand made it known that the situation at the front is so catastrophic that he would consider it a favour if the Polish units deployed immediately.

Next day the marching orders were issued to all the Polish units in readiness, or at least in a state allowing combat use. In such a way the 10th Cavalry Brigade was hastily created. In fact, the unit did not have a full brigade strength. The composition was as follows:
- a command, consisting of part of the headquarters and staff services unit;
- a tank regiment, without the second battalion, actually a tank battalion led by regiment commander;
- a motorized cavalry troop, referred to as the dragoon regiment, with two squadrons and two motorcycle platoons, one unit from each of the 24th Uhlans Regiment and the 10th Mounted Rifles Regiment;
- an anti-tank troop, with one 47 mm battery and one 25 mm squadron;
- a pioneer company;
- an anti-aircraft battery;

An American Red Cross column joined the brigade voluntarily. The column went astray after the first aircraft bombing.

Marching readiness was announced at dawn on the 9 June. The disposition and allocation were altered a few times. The brigade reached its final destination near Avize on 12 June 1940. On April

[193]: *Top left: Motorcyclists of the 10th Brigade near Montbard.*

[194]: *Top: Road congestion in front of the 10th Brigade. The young officer spearheading the column is cadet (podchorąży) Olesiński riding a Peugeot 350 cc motorcycle.*

[195]: *Middle: Anti–tank guns of the 10th Brigade at rest on a shady road.*

[196]: *Bottom: Renault R40 tank from the 2nd Battalion. The tank has an outlined tri–colour camouflage.*

87

13, at night, the unit moved near Montmort in readiness to cover the right flank of French VII Corps. A detachment of the brigade was ordered to hold Champaubert as a base of further operations. This detachment consisted of the tank platoon, the dragoon squadron, the motorcycle platoon and the 47 mm anti-tank platoon. The reconnaissance made towards Montmirail encountered German motorcycle scouts. Polish troops sustained some losses, but were able to warn the Champaubert detachment. The German attack was fended off, and two German tanks were destroyed. In the afternoon the brigade regrouped between Soizy and St.Prix, defending the Morin river. The tanks were ready to launch a counter attack from the forest near Montgivroux. The counter attack conducted in the evening, with full battalion strength, repelled the German advance. In the meantime, the neighbouring French divisions begun to retreat. The brigade could be outflanked, so on June 14 it withdrew towards Euvy-Gourgançon. The road congestion and German air activity made the task challenging. The subsequent order directed the brigade towards Chapelle. It was the last order received, from that point on all communications with the headquarters ceased.

[197]: Brigade in passing through a burning French village. The photograph shows that apart from R35 modifié 39 and R40 tanks, brigade had at least one R35 tank with short barrel cannon.

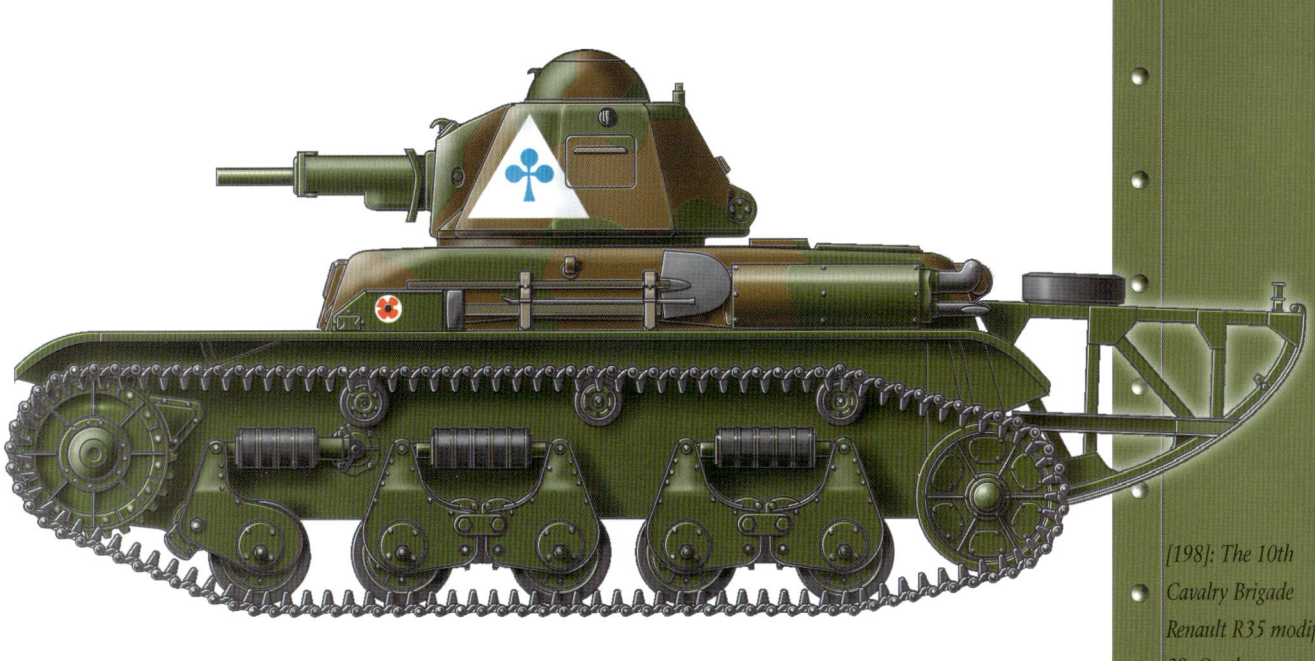

The brigade set off to secure the passage through the Channel of Burgundy. En route to Dosches and then Montbard, the brigade cooperated randomly with French units and participated in some skirmishes. In order to achieve the objective some of the vehicles had to be abandoned in the woods near Chaource. The fuel collected was then distributed between the vehicles necessary for the attack. On 16 June the brigade left the Chaource forest. Part of the column was displaced in the road congestion and never rejoined the brigade. The surprise attack on Montbard was a success. The battle was nonetheless difficult, and the fighting continued into the night 16/17 June. Unfortunately, the bridge was blown up before the brigade had an opportunity to cross it. The brigade then withdrew to Grand Jailly forest to regroup. In order to find a way out of the trap, all but three out of 17 remaining tanks had to be left behind. The number of automobiles also had to be reduced. Approximately half of the vehicles were abandoned. This provided enough fuel to cross 100 kilometres. A few additional barrels of gasoline were obtained along the way, so the remainder of the brigade reached Dijon. At Lamargette the tanks ran out of fuel. The crews set the tanks on fire and continued the journey in the automobiles. On 17 June, towards the evening, all the remaining vehicles were destroyed by their crews.

[198]: The 10th Cavalry Brigade Renault R35 modifié 39. On the turret, an identifying insignia of the French unit the tank was transferred from. On a few tanks there was a red poppy flower painted inside the flaming grenade emblem. Out of their own initiative, some crews painted this emblem to commemorate their commander General Maczek. Maczek in Polish means a small poppy flower.

[199]: Renault R35 modifié 39 tank. A Senegal soldier sits on the tail of the tank. After his unit was scattered in fighting, he joined the Polish brigade for a while.

[200]: The 10th Brigade tanks on the road through the forest. In the foreground a Renault R35 modifié 39 tank number 51519.

[201]: The tank column on the wooded path. The tank in front is a modification of the R35 referred to as Renault R35 modifié 39, The tank has a number 51530. On the right, in the background one of brigade's trucks, a Renault probably AHS type.

The 2nd Battalion, left at Camp de Satory, received its tanks after the departure of the 10th Cavalry Brigade. After just a few days, the tanks were taken back in order to re-equip the French 25th Battalion. In the following few days, the 2nd Battalion obtained new tanks from the factory. But there were only enough to equip two companies. On 10 June, the battalion was ordered to join the defences of Paris. The order was quickly recalled, and the battalion was send by rail to Fere Champenoise. The purpose was to join the 10th Brigade. Due to German bombardment and delayed train traffic, the battalion was unloaded off the train. It was to reach its destination by road. On 16 June heavy bombing from the air caused some casualties.

The battalion, now deployed as part of the French I Corps, provided an anti-tank defence along the perimeter between Velaucay and Levreux. Since the I Corps withdrew suddenly, the battalion begun a slow retreat delaying the advance of the enemy. The news that the Polish formations should attempt an evacuation to Great Britain reached the battalion. The tanks were directed towards Bayonne. The batalion was stopped along the way by the order of the 7th Army. An officer was dispatched to French headquarters to clarify the situation. The officer did not return for a few hours. In the mean time, a liaison officer from General Burhardt-Bukacki, chief of Polish Military Mission (*Polska Misja Wojskowa*) reached the battalion. The information delivered by him was that the last ship to Great Britain departs from St. Jean-de-Luz on 25 June at 13:00. The battalion commander ordered the destruction of the tanks. The battalion's personnel was loaded on the automobiles and departed. At the port all the vehicles were returned to the French authorities. The soldiers boarded the ship and arrived at Liverpool on 30 June 1940.

The 3rd and 4th Tank Battalions, still not fully organized, and the Armoured Training Centre were evacuated to Bayonne by train on 16 June. From there, they marched to St. Jean-de-Luz.

Polish transatlantic liners "Batory" and "Sobieski" took the soldiers to Great Britain. The voyage ended on 24 June 1940.

[202]: *Two of the 10th Brigade's R40 tanks, abandoned in the grove along the way, due to lack of fuel.*

[203]: *Another photograph of the R40 tanks abandoned in the grove.*

[204]: Renault R40 tanks at the edge of the forest.

[205]: Renault R40 from 10th Cavalry Brigade. Number not known. Two tone camouflage with contour lines.

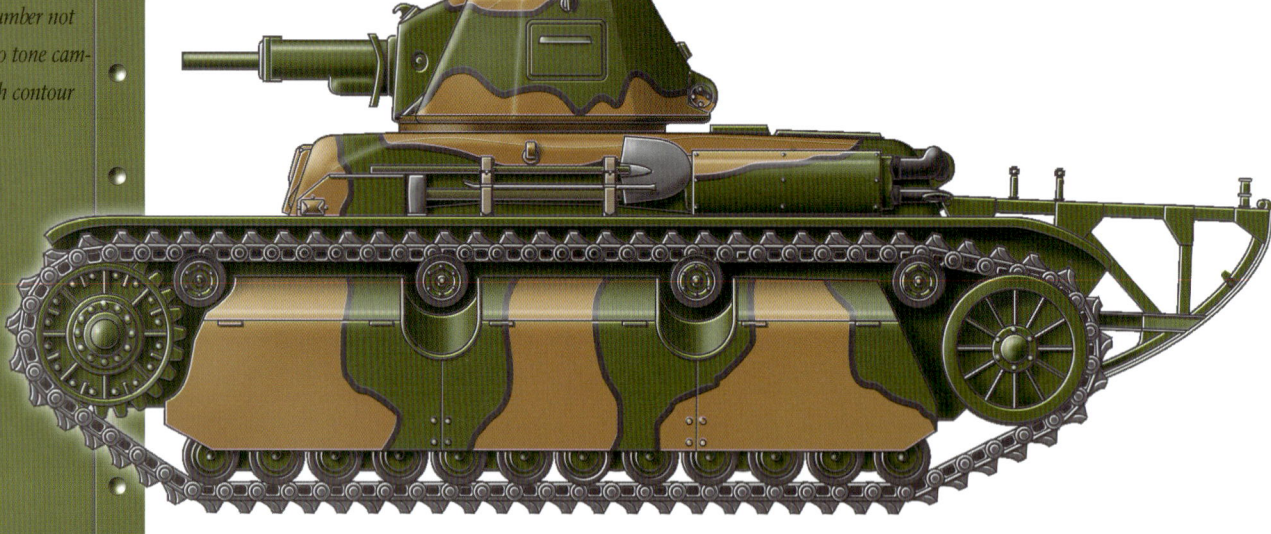

[206]: R40 equipped with a radio, with a characteristic antenna mount. Camouflage most likely two colour, spray painted without contour lines.

[207]: Brigade tanks abandoned in a clearing in the woods due to lack of fuel. The R40 tank in the foreground had number 51669.

[208]: Another view of the R40 tanks abandoned in a glade, closest tank is 51669, the tank to the left 51679.

[209]: Photograph of the same clearing from more distant perspective. On the right one more R40 tank.

[210]: The road leading from the woods to the glade where the tanks were abandoned.

[211]: R40 tank number 51651, in the background 51669.

[212]: Two R40 tanks.

[213]: R40 tanks in German hands.

[214]: Next to the Hotchkiss tank, Polish Renault R40 number 51669.

[215]: German staging area for captured equipment. German soldiers are posing on R40 number 51670 from Polish 10th Cavalry Brigade.

95

Badges

[1, 1a]: Tank officer badge, the obverse and the reverse. The badge was officially approved by the War Ministry's (Ministerstwo Spraw Wojskowych) order number 25, issued 5 August 1925. Size 42 by 26 mm. (From the collection of Tomasz Marszałek)

[2, 2a]: 1st Tank Regiment Poznań. The obverse and the reverse of the badge established by War Ministry's order number 49, dating from 13 December 1921. Size 55 by 30 mm. (From the collection of The Polish Institute and Sikorski Museum)

[3, 3a]: Armoured Badge, the front side and the stud nut. The badge issued in accordance with War Ministry's order number 20 dated 3 November 1932. Manufactured by W. Gontarczyk. (From the collection of Tomasz Marszałek)

[4]: Armoured Badge. Size 30 by 35 mm. Unknown manufacturer (From the collection of Polish Army Museum – Muzeum Wojska Polskiego)

[5a, 5b]: 2nd Armoured Battalion Żurawica, the obverse and the reverse of the badge. A version with a large armoured insignia. Size 37 by 37 mm. Manufactured by B. Grabski. (From the collection of Tomasz Marszałek)

[6a, 6b, 6c]: 2nd Armoured Battalion Żurawica, the obverse, the reverse and the stud nut. Variation of the badge with a small armoured insignia. Size 39 by 39 mm. Manufactured by B. Grabski. (From the collection of Tomasz Marszałek)

[7]: 2nd Armoured Battalion Żurawica badge. Size 39 by 39 mm. Manufactured by W. Gontarczyk. (from the collection of Piła Regional Museum - Muzeum Okręgowe Piła)

[8]: 2nd Armoured Battalion Żurawica badge. Enlisted men version. Size 39 by 39 mm. Manufacturer unknown. (Private collection)

[9a, 9b, 9c]: 12th Armoured Battalion Łuck, the obverse, the reverse and the stud nut. Size 40 by 40 mm. Manufactured by W. Miecznik. (From the collection of Tomasz Marszałek)